THE
END
FROM THE
BEGINNING

BY JOHN

Cover design and text composition by Tara Gieck

2009 10 11 12 13 14 · 5 4 3 2 1

Copyright © 2009 by John
ISBN-13: 978-1-57258-601-7
ISBN-10: 1-57258-601-X
Library of Congress Control Number: 2009925050

www.endfromthebeginning.com

Published by

TEACH Services, Inc.
www.TEACHServices.com

THE END FROM THE BEGINNING

Table of Contents

THE END FROM THE BEGINNING

Preface

My dearly beloved and longed for brethren in Christ Jesus,

The book you hold in your hands is written to edify, encourage, and challenge you. It is meant first and foremost to point you to Jesus Christ, the only Savior, and to give you a deeper, abiding confidence in the Holy Bible as the inspired word of God.

As you read through this book, you will find things that will delight your soul. You will find things that will cause you to kneel in amazement at the incredible mercy and truth of God. You will find things that may be new and unfamiliar to you. I urge you, please, to be as were our brethren the Bereans who searched the Scriptures to see if the things which were shared with them were true.

You will note that the literary style I choose to convey the thoughts in this book appear similar to Scripture itself. Indeed, a majority of *The End from the Beginning* is actually quotations from the Holy Bible. For all verses, those that are quoted in their entirety as well as those that only partially cited, the Scripture reference appears in the footnotes. Please refer to the Bible itself and cross-reference the verses that appear in this work. Search the Scriptures.[1] Test all things; hold fast what is good.[2]

I want to be very clear at the outset of this work that I do not claim to have a prophetic gift. This book is not intended to be considered a continuation of the Bible, nor is this in any way a supernaturally produced manuscript. The thoughts that are shared here come from my personal study of the Scriptures, and from a deep conviction that the church needs to turn away from the world and return to a diligent study of the Holy Bible.

You and I may disagree on some of the points shared in this book. That is to be expected.

1 *John 5:39, 40*
2 *I Thess. 5:21*

Nevertheless, if *The End from the Beginning* causes your faith in the Author of the Holy Bible to be strengthened, leads you to search its sacred pages more thoroughly, and deepens your commitment to Jesus Christ, it will have accomplished its purpose.

May the God who is Truth lead you into all truth; may the grace of the Savior who died for you cause you to live for Him; and may the Holy Spirit sanctify you wholly in preparation for entrance into the eternal kingdom of love, joy and peace.

Faithfully,
John

THE END FROM THE BEGINNING

Introduction

In the beginning God declared what would be in the end. And from the beginning unto the end, God is love.[1]

God sees the end from the beginning. The past and the future are equally clear to Him who controls the present. He knows the depths of darkness and depravity caused by sin; He knows the height of light and glory to come in the redemption offered through His blood. He is patient in waiting for the fulfillment of His plan, formed before the creation of the world,[2] to restore us and the entire universe. He knows the time for all things.

As it is written, to everything there is a season, a time for every purpose under heaven: a time to be born, and a time to die; a time to plant, and a time to pluck what is planted; a time to kill, and a time to heal; a time to break down, and a time to build up; a time to weep, and a time to laugh;... a time to love, and a time to hate; a time of war, and a time of peace;... a time to keep silence, and a time to speak.[3] In such a time as this, we must speak the truth in love;[4] we must share the truth as it is in Jesus.[5]

The Bible speaks to those who are called to preach the truth in Jesus. It declares that we will be opposed, derided as fanatical, and some will even have to lay down their lives. The Word of God tells us that if we faint in the day of adversity, our strength is small. We must deliver those who are drawn toward death, and hold back those stumbling to the slaughter. If we say, Surely we did not know this, does not He who weighs the hearts consider it? He who keeps your soul, does He not know it? And will He not render to each man according to his deeds?[6]

Therefore, my beloved in Christ Jesus, I share with you of the

---

1 I John 4:8
2 Revelation 13:8; 17:8

3 Ecclesiastes 3:1-4, 8, 7
4 Ephesians 4:15
5 Ephesians 4:21
6 Proverbs 24:10-12

plan of salvation and prophetic messages revealed in the Holy Bible. Hidden mysteries clouded in superstition are unveiled in the Word of God. Search the Scriptures and you will find Christ, and in finding Him, you will find life.[7]

However, I know that some will reject what is written, even those who take the name of Christ. Many will, like the ancients of Israel, scorn the counsel of truth in Scriptures. Sadly, many shepherds are blind guides that are satisfied with their traditions and rituals, and will fight against the message of repentance and mercy given that man might be spared the wrath of God. Indeed, there are those that will clamor for my head because I speak the truth, even as they have stoned the prophets of old, sawn asunder those who faithfully rebuked them,[8] and crucified the Lord of glory. But know for certain that if you put me to death, you will surely bring innocent blood on yourselves; for truly the Lord has sent me to you to speak all these words in your hearing.[9]

---

7 John 5:39,40
8 Matthew 23:34; Hebrews 11:35-37
9 Jeremiah 26:15

Chapter One

PROPHETIC WORD MADE MORE SURE

John, servant of Jesus Christ, to all the saints in Christ Jesus who are scattered across the globe, to those in Babylon and those that are free: Grace to you and peace from God our Father and the Lord Jesus Christ.

I thank my God upon every remembrance of you, always in every prayer of mine making request for you all with joy, for your fellowship in the gospel from the first day until now, being confident of this very thing, that He who has begun a good work in you will complete it until the day of Jesus Christ.[1]

Beloved, I pray that your love may abound still more and more in knowledge and all discernment, and that you may approve the things that are excellent,[2] true, and trustworthy.

Inasmuch as many have taken in hand to set in order a narrative of those things which will be fulfilled in the future among us, just as those who from the beginning were eyewitnesses and ministers of the word delivered to them for us, it seemed good to me also, having learned that all which is written in the Word is faithful and true, to write to you an orderly account of things that shall be hereafter, that you may know the certainty of those things in which you were instructed,[3] and the truth of those things which will shortly come to pass.

I write to you that you might know Him who declares the end from the beginning, and from ancient times things that are not yet done, saying, 'My counsel shall stand, and I will do all My pleasure.'[4] Our heavenly Father declares the future to His children, for surely the Lord God does nothing, unless He reveals His secret to His servants the prophets.[5] And

---

1 *Phil. 1:1-6*
2 *Phil. 1:8-9*

3 *Luke 1:1-4*
4 *Isa. 46:10*
5 *Amos 3:7*

so we have the prophetic word confirmed, which you do well to heed as a light that shines in a dark place, until the day dawns and the morning star rises in your hearts; knowing this first, that no prophecy of Scripture is of any private interpretation, for prophecy never came by the will of man, but holy men of God spoke as they were moved by the Holy Spirit.[6]

Therefore, we give thanks unto God for His Word and for the promise of eternal life in Christ Jesus. In this life we give thanks for the hope that we have in Him, and also because He reveals the future to us through His Word. You know and can see that our salvation is nearer than when we first believed,[7] and soon we shall behold Him who is the Desire of Nations.[8] I pray that you will stand in that day,[9] and that you will be assured of the things which I write unto you.

Fellow pilgrims, I tell you now, as you have been told before, take heed that no one deceives you. For many will come in the name of Jesus, declaring that He is the Christ, and will deceive many.[10] They will deceive, not a few, but many.

We are indeed in the last days. The time has come that many do not endure sound doctrine, but according to their own desires, because they have itching ears, they heap up for themselves teachers; and they turn their ears away from the truth, and are turned aside to fables.[11] These are they who would rather be entertained by pseudo-Christian novels and supposed Christian movies than to search the Word for truth. But take heed; see, I have told you all things beforehand.[12]

Little children, it is the last hour; and as you have heard that the Antichrist is coming, even now many antichrists have come, by which we know that it is the last hour. They went out from us, but they were not of us; for if they had been of us, they would have continued with us; but they went out that they might be made manifest, that none of them were of us.

---

6 II Peter 1:19-21
7 Romans 13:11
8 Haggai 2:7
9 Eph. 6:13

10 Matt 24:4-5
11 II Tim. 4:3-4
12 Mark 13:23

But you have an anointing from the Holy One, and you know all things. I have not written to you because you do not know the truth, but because you know it, and that no lie is of the truth.[13]

I, John, the servant of Christ Jesus, seek to make known to you mysteries hidden from the foundation of the world. These things were not made known unto me by some extraordinary revelation, but through the same means available to us all: the indwelling of the Holy Spirit giving light to the Holy Bible which God gives to those that long to know and do His will. Blessed is he who reads and those who hear the words of this prophecy, and keep those things which are written in it; for the time is near.[14]

For this reason I became a minister according to the gift of the grace of God given to me by the effective working of His power. To me, who am less than the least of all the saints, this grace was given, that I should preach among you the unsearchable riches of Christ, and to make all see what is the fellowship of the mystery, which from the beginning of the ages has been hidden in God who created all things through Jesus Christ; to the intent that now the manifold wisdom of God might be made known by the church to the principalities and powers in the heavenly places.[15]

My beloved in the Lord, I earnestly pray that you will give thought to the word which is shared here. Do not quench the Spirit. Do not despise prophecies. Test all things; hold fast what is good.

Now may the God of peace Himself sanctify you completely; and may your whole spirit, soul, and body be preserved blameless at the coming of our Lord Jesus Christ. He who calls you is faithful, who also will do it. Brethren, pray for me.

I charge you by the Lord that this epistle be read to all the holy brethren. The grace of our Lord Jesus Christ be with you. Amen[16].

---

13 *I John 2:18-21*
14 *Rev. 1:3*

15 *Eph. 3:1, 4-10*
16 *I Thess. 5:19-21, 23-24, 25, 27-28*

Chapter Two

FROM THE FOUNDATION OF THE WORLD

In the beginning was the Word, and the Word was with God, and the Word was God. He was in the beginning with God.[1]

God was, is, and always will be. The Word declares, I am the Alpha and the Omega, the Beginning and the End, the First and the Last. Blessed are those who do His commandments.[2] He who is from the beginning knows the end, and He who reveals the end from the beginning promises to be with us even to the end of the world.[3]

In the beginning God created the heavens and the earth.[4] God formed this world consistent with the principles of His kingdom in heaven. His government is founded on truth, righteousness, and love. His throne is established upon mercy,[5] and His commandments are holy, and just, and good.[6] At the time of creation, all that was formed in this world revealed that God is love.[7]

The guiding principle of the kingdom of God, which is a reflection of the character of God, is self-sacrificing love. Throughout the universe, all were to render obedience and service, not out of fear, but in love to God; perfect love casts out fear.[8] God demonstrated His own love toward us, in that while we were still sinners, Christ died for us.[9] Therefore, we love Him, because He first loved us.[10]

At the time of creation, God spoke the Word, and it was; for the kingdom of God is not only in word, but in power.[11] It was by the Word that all

---

1 John 1:1-2
2 Rev. 22:13,14
3 Matt. 28:20
4 Gen. 1:1

5 Isa. 16:5
6 Romans 7:12
7 I John 4:16
8 I John 4:18
9 Romans 5:8
10 I John 4:19
11 I Cor. 4:20

things were created. He is the image of the invisible God, the firstborn over all creation. For by Him all things were created that are in heaven and that are on earth, visible and invisible, whether thrones or dominions or principalities or powers. All things were created through Him and for Him. And He is before all things, and in Him all things consist.[12]

God, who at various times and in various ways spoke in time past to the fathers by the prophets, has in these last days spoken to us by His Son, whom He has appointed heir of all things, through whom also He made the worlds; who being the brightness of His glory and the express image of His person, and upholding all things by the word of His power, when He had by Himself purged our sins, sat down at the right hand of the Majesty on high.[13]

Beloved, consider the incredible love of God. From the beginning, the Word, Jesus

Christ, God in the flesh, was our Creator. It was He who spoke, and the world came into being. It is He who, through the Word of His power, upholds the world. It will be He who, at His coming in glory, reigns over the kingdom of God.

He, Jesus Christ, is the Lamb slain from the foundation of the world.[14] Before the creation of the world, He knew that He would have to suffer on the cruel cross of Calvary. Before the beginning of life on this planet, He knew that the end of His life would be at the hands of those He had created. Before He spoke the Word and it was, He knew that He, the sinless One, would be condemned by guilty man to taste death for our sakes.[15] Yet still He created this world!

Truly, God is love.[16] Gaze upon the majestic snowcapped mountains in the winter, rising in glory and power unto the heavens. Smell the fragrance of a crimson rose blossoming

---

12 *Col. 1:16-17*
13 *Heb. 1:1-3*

14 *Rev. 13:8*
15 *Heb. 2:9*
16 *I John 4:8*

in the spring. Feel the cool, soft breeze caress your face on a warm summer day. Bask in the multi-colored canvas of the trees on a crisp fall afternoon. Each of these beauties of nature testifies of the love of God for His creatures.

Closer to the heart, God draws us in love to Him through our relationships with each other. An innocent child looks up to its father and discerns trust and comfort. An awestruck youth peers into the heart of another and envisions a lifetime of endless possibilities. An exhausted mother looks into the eyes of her newborn child and imagines a future of joy and hope. The tear-stained eyes of the aged staring at the silent form of a much-loved spouse witness to memories of care and tenderness. Even the grave reveals the love of God for us; even death…

Behold the Lamb of God who takes away the sin of the world![17] Look upon the Son of God as He is led up the Place of the Skull. His back is lacerated, striped by the cords of leather embedded with glass and iron.[18] He stumbles along the path under the weight of the cross. Blood flows from His brow where a crown of thorns pierces His skin. Arriving at the summit of Calvary, He lies down, and is silent, as the soldier pummels the nails into His hands and feet. The living Word of God speaks: Father, forgive them, for they do not know what they do.[19]

The King of the universe hangs suspended between heaven and earth, the Sacrifice for the transgression of the law of God. The priests spit upon Him, taunting His claims to divinity. His disciples cower in fear at the back of the crowd of mockers who look on with fiendish delight. Under the tremendous pressure of carrying the sins of the world, His heart breaks and He cries out: My God, My God, why have You forsaken Me?[20] Father, into Your hands I commit My spirit.[21] It is finished![22]

---

17 John 1:29

18 Mark 15:15
19 Luke 23:34
20 Matt 27:46
21 Luke 23:46
22 John 19:30

Dear beloved, I urge you, please, if you have not yet asked this Man who is God, Jesus Christ, the crucified and resurrected One, to be your Savior, please invite Him into your heart, mind and life right now. Breathe a prayer, crying out to God in repentance and gratitude that you can be forgiven, healed, redeemed, and made whole through the blood of the Lamb. Please, bow before Him and ask Him for a new life – a life of faith and love – trusting completely in the Son of God for your eternal salvation.

Behold the Man![23]

---

23 John 19:5

Chapter Three

THAT IT MIGHT BE FULFILLED

The Elder, to the elect lady and her children, whom I love in truth, and not only I, but also all those who have known the truth, because of the truth which abides in us and will be with us forever: Grace, mercy, and peace will be with you from God the Father and from the Lord Jesus Christ, the Son of the Father, in truth and love.[1]

Christ Jesus came to His own, and His own did not receive Him.[2] He was despised and rejected of men[3] because men loved darkness rather than light, because their deeds were evil. For everyone practicing evil hates the light and does not come to the light, lest his deeds should be exposed. But he who does the truth comes to the light.[4]

God came to be with us, Immanuel, Christ Jesus, so that we might know and love God. In Him dwells all the fullness of the Godhead bodily.[5] He came not only to preach the gospel,[6] but to establish the kingdom of God.[7] He is the Priest; He is the Sacrifice. He is the King; He is the Servant. He is the Prophet; He is the fulfillment of prophecy. Jesus Christ understood that the establishment of the kingdom of God was only possible through His consenting to wear a crown of thorns and to suffer an ignominious death on the cross.

Although Jesus was the Son of God, yet He learned obedience by the things which He suffered.[8] Christ was born to die. God died as a man, that man might

---

1 II John 1-3
2 John 1:11
3 Isa. 53:3
4 John 3:19-21

5 Col. 2:9
6 Mark 1:15
7 Isa. 9:6,7
8 Heb. 5:8

live with God. Knowing that He was appointed to die, He came into this world to conquer sin and death.

It was by love that He was sent to this world;[9] it was by faith that He went to the cross. It is by love that we are drawn to the cross; it is by faith that we gain the victory over the world.[10]

My brethren, to understand love and faith, consider the cross of our Savior. His faith took Him up Golgotha; His love bound Him to the cross. Love is not feeling; it is choice. Faith is not blind; it is seeing the invisible.[11] The Savior chose to go to the cross because of His love for us and because of His faith in the Word.

The Holy Scriptures opened to Jesus, and reveal to us, that He is the Anointed One. The Word testifies that Jesus is the Son of man;[12] His Father testifies that Christ is the Son of God.[13]

Christ gained the faith and courage to march to the place of His crucifixion an innocent and willing Sacrifice through His confidence in the promises of God. He had come to know and believe the love that His Father has for Him,[14] and that truly we, too, must live by faith in every word that proceeds from the mouth of God.[15]

Jesus understood that He had come as the Seed of the woman to crush the head of the serpent, knowing that in the process He would undergo a bruise Himself.[16] The seed of Abraham, Isaac, and Jacob,[17] Jesus descended from the tribe of Judah.[18] He was of the royal line of David,[19] yet Jesus Himself said that His kingdom was not of this world.[20] He believed that He was indeed born of a virgin,[21] that an angel had named Him Jesus, and therefore He chose to believe that He shall save His people from their sins.[22]

---

9 John 3:16
10 I John 5:4
11 Heb. 11:1
12 Dan.7:13
13 Psalm 2:7; Matt. 3:17, 17:5;
   Mark 9:7; Luke 9:35; II Peter 1:17
14 I John 4:16
15 Deut. 8:3; Matt. 4:4
16 Gen. 3:14, 15
17 Gen. 17:7, 21:12, 28:14; Matt. 1:2
18 Gen. 49:10; Luke 1:32
19 II Sam. 7:12; Luke 2:4
20 John 18:36
21 Isa. 7:14; Matt. 1:23
22 Luke 1:31; Matt. 1:21

Jesus is the Fulfillment

Prophecy from Old Testament	Fulfillment in Jesus' Life
A Saviour to come crush out the power of Satan *Genesis 3:14, 15*	*Galatians 4:4,5*
To come from the tribe of Judah *Genesis 49:8-10*	*Luke 3:23, 33, 34*
A star to appear at the arrival of the King *Numbers 24:17*	*Matthew 2:1,2*
To be born of a virgin *Isaiah 7:14*	*Matthew 1:18, 21-25*
To be born in the city of Bethlehem *Micah 5:2*	*Luke 2:4-7*
Betrayed for 30 pieces of silver *Zechariah 11:12,13*	*Matthew 27:3-7*
Would be spat upon and beaten *Isaiah 50:6*	*Matthew 26:67, 68*
His side is pierced *Zechariah 12:10*	*John 19:34*
To be mocked by those around Him *Psalm 22:7,8*	*Matthew 27:41-43*
He cries out to His Father in heaven *Psalm 22:1*	*Matthew 27:46*
Will have His hands and feet pierced *Psalm 22:16*	*Luke 23:33*
He suffered for us and our sins *Isaiah 53:3-5*	*Matthew 27:38-43*
He is buried with the rich *Isaiah 53:9*	*Matthew 27:57-60*
He will rise again! *Psalm 16:9,10*	*Mark 16:6,7*
He is resurrected on the third day *Hosea 6:1,2*	*Luke 23:54-56; 24:1-6*

The Holy Spirit illumined the mind of Jesus to the truth of the Bible, even as He will do for us when we ask.[23] Jesus learned that it was prophesied that the Messiah would be born in Bethlehem Ephrata;[24] He was informed that the entire Roman Empire was numbered so that the holy One could arrive in the City of David in time for His birth in a stable.[25] He heard that, in fulfillment of the Word, an angelic star shone brightly, announcing His incarnation.[26] He was told that a prophet and a prophetess declared Him to be the Christ when He was dedicated in the temple,[27] and that wise men came from Sheba, Midian, and Seba[28] bearing gifts at His birth. These gifts sustained Jesus and His mother and Joseph when, consistent with what had been written,[29] they fled in the night to Egypt because His life was endangered.[30] They later returned to Israel and settled in Nazareth, not Bethlehem, that it might be fulfilled what was spoken by the prophets.[31] And the Child grew and became strong in spirit, filled with wisdom; and the grace of God was upon Him.[32]

From His childhood Jesus stored up the Word of God in His heart and was obedient to His parents.[33] According to the custom of His time, upon entering manhood Jesus went up to the temple at Jerusalem for the Passover feast.[34] Imagine His horror when He witnessed the shedding of the blood of the innocent victim on behalf of the sinner, and at twelve years of age He realized that He was the Lamb of God.[35] Even as a young man, Jesus of Nazareth understood His unique relation to God and comprehended the work that His heavenly Father entrusted to His only begotten Son.[36] As He became older, Jesus increased in wisdom and stature, and in favor with God and men.[37]

---

23 *John 16:13*
24 *Micah 5:2*
25 *Luke 2:4-7*
26 *Num. 24:17; Matt. 2:2*
27 *Luke 2:25-38*
28 *Psalms 72:10; Isa. 60:6*
29 *Hosea 11:1*
30 *Matt. 2:13-15*

31 *Judges 13:5; Matt. 2:23*
32 *Luke 2:40*
33 *Psalm 119:9,11; Luke 2:51*
34 *Luke 2:42*
35 *Isa. 53:7; John 1:36*
36 *Luke 2:49*
37 *Luke 2:52*

Since all these prophecies about His birth and life were fulfilled, the Son of God knew that the prophecies about His death would also be fulfilled. Beloved, understand this wonderful truth: the prophecies concerning the death of Christ were fulfilled only because Jesus chose to participate in the will of God. He could have said No, and we would have all been lost. Thanks be to God for His unspeakable gift,[38] Jesus Christ, the living Word of God!

God is love, and love requires freedom. His Father gave Jesus the choice whether He would accept His role as the Sacrifice for the sins of the world. Even so, God gives us the choice whether we will be the heirs of eternal life through faith. Jesus chose to surrender His will to the Father because of His love and faith. O that we might live for Him, and even die for Him, in love and faith.

As He practiced His trade as a humble carpenter in Nazareth, Jesus grew to realize the plans that God had for Him. Not only was it prophesied concerning His birth and how He should live, but also how Jesus would die in the appointed manner and time[39] planned for Him from before the foundation of the world.[40]

He knew that when the time came, He would ride triumphantly as Messiah into Jerusalem on the back of a donkey.[41] Nevertheless, He recognized that before the heavenly crown must come the earthly cross. He read the Scriptures that foretold, not an immediate glorious earthly reign with His family, but an estrangement from all who called Him brother.[42] He anticipated, not a throne of gold and ivory, but a betrayal by a so-called friend[43] for a mere thirty pieces of silver,[44] the price of a common slave.[45] He also realized that when He was led as a lamb to the slaughter,[46]

---

38 II Corinthians 9:15

39 Gal. 4:4
40 Rev. 13:8
41 Zech. 9:9; Matt. 21:5
42 Psalm 69:8; John 7:5
43 Psalm 41:9, 55:12-14; John 13:18
44 Zech. 11:12; Matt. 26:15, 27:3-10
45 Exodus 21:32
46 Isa. 53:7

THAT IT MIGHT BE FULFILLED

those who had called Him Master in times of glory and fame would flee and leave Him alone.[47] Alone to bear the sins of the world.

Jesus knew that eventually He would have to face sin-infested men, possessed by demonic forces, who would take Him prisoner and subject Him to the worst travesty of justice known in history. Through the Word of God Christ learned that after He completed His ministry of teaching and healing, His human form would be crushed in insufferable anguish. He would be struck in the head many times;[48] He would endure merciless whipping across His back; His beard would be pulled out from the roots; men would repeatedly spit in His face.[49] By the time His tormentors were finished, He would be marred more than any man had ever been.[50] Jesus would become almost unrecognizable.

O beloved brethren, consider the agony that our dear Jesus endured for our salvation! He knew that He would have to taste the depths of hell that we might gain heaven. He knew all this before Gethsemane; He understood all these things before He trod the path to Calvary. Knowing all this, He pressed forward to the pinnacle of shame and torment that He might conquer death and sin through faith and love.

Think about this: all the while that He planed the wood and hammered the nails in the carpenter's shop, Jesus knew that someday He would be stretched out on a wooden instrument of torture and have nails pierce His hands of blessing. All the while that He healed the sick, cured the demoniacs, and gave sight to the blind, He knew that soon He would be lifted up[51] and mocked by the creatures He had come to save.

Jesus was despised and rejected by men, a Man of sorrows and

47 Zech. 13:7; Mark 14:27
48 Micah 5:1; Matt. 27:30
49 Isa. 50:6; Matt. 26:67, 27:26
50 Isa. 52:14

51 John 12:32

acquainted with grief. And we hid, as it were, our faces from Him; He was despised, and we did not esteem Him. Surely He has borne our griefs and carried our sorrows; yet we esteemed Him stricken, smitten by God, and afflicted. But He was wounded for our transgressions, He was bruised for our iniquities; the chastisement for our peace was upon Him, and by His stripes we are healed.[52]

When Jesus looked into eternity, the Word of God revealed a glorious future and a heavenly kingdom. Yet there is only one entrance into the kingdom: by way of crucifixion. Jesus knew that His Father spoke to Him when He read: Kings shall see and arise, princes also shall worship, because of the Lord who is faithful, the Holy One of Israel; and He has chosen You.[53]

He was truly the Chosen One. He chose to believe in the Word of God. Jesus chose to travel to the Place of the Skull and to erect a monument to the love and faithfulness of God for the entire universe to behold.

Looking into the near future, Jesus saw that much of His family would disown Him, His friends disappoint Him, and His enemies sneer at Him while He hung on the cross. Jesus would be tempted to turn back, but He would press forward to the cross of shame. He would not fail nor be discouraged until He accomplished His Father's will.[54] Indeed, when the time had come for Him to be received up, He steadfastly set His face to go to Jerusalem.[55]

From the outset of His earthly ministry, Jesus saw that He would have to often cleanse the temple from the defilement of the self-serving prelates at the conclusion of His earthly life.[56] He would have a final Passover feast with His disciples[57] and then be betrayed by one who had broken bread with Him.[58] Christ knew that He would not be the only one who hung on a tree that day. His betrayer

---

52 Isa. 53:2-5; Matt. 8:17
53 Isa. 49:7; Matt. 26:67

54 Isa. 42:2-4
55 Luke 9:51
56 Matt. 21:12, 13
57 Luke 21:15
58 Psalm 41:9; John 13:18

would take his own life by hanging himself.[59] From the Last Supper to Gethsemane, from the Judgment Hall to Calvary, Jesus knew the end from the beginning, and still He went forward in faith and love to His final hours of torment and triumph.

Long before He went up to Jerusalem that week, Jesus knew that He would be flogged and beaten. He anticipated lying down on the crossbeams of history and having His hands and feet pierced.[60] He read in the Scriptures that when parched with sorrow, He who had changed water into wine[61] would be given bitter vinegar to quench His thirst.

Indeed, He knew that when that dreadful day came, He would look for someone to take pity upon Him, and there would be no one with compassion there to relieve His agony.[62] No one.

All we like sheep have gone astray; we have turned, every one, to his own way; and the Lord has laid on Him the iniquity of us all. He was oppressed and He was afflicted, yet He opened not His mouth; He was led as a lamb to the slaughter, and as a sheep before its shearers is silent, so He opened not His mouth.[63]

When Christ was in the judgment hall, when He was being flayed, when He willingly offered Himself on Calvary, He did not revile His assassins. Instead, He prayed: Father, forgive them, for they do not know what they do.[64] Jesus knew in advance that it would not be the last prayer He offered that day.

As He studied the Scriptures in His youth and early manhood, Christ came to realize what would take place on the day He demonstrated the unfathomable love of God to the universe. He foresaw the people gathered about the cross mocking Him, shaking their heads and saying: He trusted in God; let Him deliver Him now if He will have Him; for He said, 'I am the Son of God.'[65] Jesus envisioned the

---

59 Matt. 27:4, 5
60 Psalm 22:16; Luke 23:33
61 John 2:7-9
62 Psalm 69:20, 21; John 19:28-30

63 Isa. 53:6, 7; Acts 8:32.
64 Luke 23:34
65 Psalm 22:7, 8; Matt. 27:43

soldiers ridiculing Him as they divided His garments among them and cast lots for His clothing.[66] He knew that, just like the Passover lamb that was slain on the night the Israelites were set free from their bondage over fifteen hundred years earlier, not one of His bones would be broken.[67] He expected to be gawked over by those who thrust His flesh through with a spear, because it was written in the Word of God.[68]

Elect brethren in the truth, our dear Savior Jesus knew all these things beforehand because He studied the Bible. His faith led Him to believe that these things were true; His love led Him to accept His position as our Sacrifice.

Yet there was something that He could not understand before He went to the garden on the night of His arrest. Jesus Christ, the Holy One of God, sinless and pure, could not foresee the hideous nature of sin. He had never transgressed the law of God, and so He never knew the distress of guilt. Therefore,

before His last night when He surrendered up His will completely, He could not have known the sorrow He would experience when the presence of His Father was withdrawn from Him. Jesus could not have anticipated the horrors of iniquity that ripped apart His breast as He hung suspended between heaven and earth and the favor of God was removed. It was because His Father allowed His Son to become sin for us[69] that Christ cried out, My God, My God, why have You forsaken Me?[70]

Amidst the darkness and gloom of the cross, Jesus could not see through the other side of the tomb. His victory over death and the grave was obscured by the weight of the sins of the world. And so it was that Jesus overcame in the same manner that we must overcome: by faith and love. Although He is the Son of God, Christ Jesus lived and died as the Son of Man.

Before He entered into His ministry, before He died, Jesus knew that He would be buried

---

66 *Psalm 22:18; Matt. 27:35*
67 *Ex. 12:46; Num. 9:12; Ps. 34:20;*
   John 19:36
68 *Zech. 12:10; John 19:37*

69 *II Corinthians 5:21*
70 *Psalm 22:1; Mark 15:34*

in the grave of a rich man; not because He made prior arrangements, but because it was written in the Scriptures.[71] However, while hanging on the cross Jesus was not worried about where He would be buried. Rather, He recounted in His mind the promises in the Word of God that portray the hope of His resurrection. His hope is our hope.

At the same time that these promises came to His mind, the terrible burden of the collective guilt of humanity pressed upon His soul. Even though the Bible declares that His flesh would not be corrupted and that He would not remain in the grave,[72] as He experienced the terrible effects of sin, Jesus was tempted to wonder whether He would indeed rise again. Jesus Himself had told His disciples that as Jonah had been in the belly of the great fish for three days, so too would He be in the heart of the earth – in the grave – three days.[73] Christ believed that He would be revived and raised up in three days because it was written that God

would do so.[74] Yet for Him to believe this was an act of faith, even as the hope of eternal life in Christ is an act of faith for us.

Although as God He knows the end from the beginning, as man Jesus had to trust in the written Word of God in the face of His present sufferings. Jesus could not use His divine power while on the cross and look into the future; that would have been sin. Instead, during the days of His flesh, when He had offered up prayers and supplications with vehement cries and tears, Jesus was saved from eternal death because of His godly fear.[75] He was saved from death because of His obedience, faith, and love. What makes His sacrifice even more amazing is that Jesus not only tasted death for each one of us,[76] but He was prepared to sacrifice His very existence – to experience the second death[77] – that we might be saved.

Dear children begotten of the Word, our hearts should burn

---

71 Isa. 53:9; Matt. 27:57-58, 60
72 Ps. 16:10, 49:15; Isa. 26:19; Acts 2:27, 31, 13:35
73 Jonah 1:17, Matt. 12:40

74 Hosea 6:1, 2; I Cor. 15:4
75 Hebrews 5:7
76 Hebrews 2:9
77 Revelation 20:6, 14

within us[78] as we consider the tremendous love of God in giving us His Son. We should slip to our knees in worship when we contemplate what Jesus endured for our salvation. Jesus looked by faith to His ascension from the grave and the earth,[79] yet His heavenly hope was rooted and grounded in the Word of God, the very same promises that we now possess.

It was by faith in the Word that He established the kingdom. It was by love that He became the Lamb of God who now ministers as High Priest in heaven above. It is by His power through the Holy Spirit that we can look into the future with confidence, knowing that by faith and love, we too shall overcome.

Amen!

---

78 *Luke 24:32*
79 *Psalm 68:18; Acts 1:9, 33*

IN THE FULLNESS OF TIME

John, to the seven churches which are throughout the world: Grace to you and peace from Him who is and who was and who is to come, and from the seven Spirits who are before His throne, and from Jesus Christ, the faithful witness, the firstborn from the dead, and the ruler over the kings of the earth. To Him who loved us and washed us from our sins in His own blood, and has made us kings and priests to His God and Father, to Him be glory and dominion forever and ever. Amen.[1]

Beloved, it would be good for us to understand how Jesus Christ, Son of God and Son of man, learned that His time had come. We, too, need to understand the times in which we live, and of the time of His second coming, for the time is at hand.[2] Indeed,

God has appointed the times and places for all men, that each might seek after God and find Him.[3] Let us trust in His promise to give us wisdom[4] and search out these secrets that God seeks to reveal to us. For to you it has been given to know the mysteries of the kingdom of God, but to the rest it is given in parables, that seeing they may not see, and hearing they may not understand.[5]

When He was about thirty years of age,[6] Jesus came to be baptized at the hands of His cousin, John the Baptist.[7] John had been preaching a baptism of repentance on the banks of the Jordan River, called of God to prepare the way for the coming of the Messiah.[8] The message of John was not popular with the reigning authority, and so he was

1 *Revelation 1:4-6*
2 *Revelation 1:3*

3 *Acts 17:26, 27*
4 *James 1:5, 6*
5 *Luke 8:10*
6 *Luke 3:23*
7 *Luke 1:36, 3:21*
8 *Luke 3:2-4*

imprisoned.[9] It was then that Jesus began preaching the gospel of the kingdom of God, and saying, The time is fulfilled, and the kingdom of God is at hand. Repent, and believe in the gospel.[10]

It is written that when the fullness of time had come, God sent forth His Son, born of a woman, born under the law, to redeem those who were under the law, that we might receive the adoption as sons.[11] The time had come for the Seed of the woman to come and trample upon the head of the serpent.[12] The time had come for redemption.

Elect according to the foreknowledge of God, you know that there are some things hard to understand in the Scriptures;[13] the manner and timing of the first advent of our Lord Jesus Christ is such a hard thing. The wicked shall do wickedly and shall not understand; yet those who are wise will understand.[14] The fear of the Lord is the beginning of wisdom; a good understanding have all those who do His commandments.[15] And so I pray that you who are sanctified by the blood of the holy Son of God may be filled with the knowledge of His will in all wisdom and spiritual understanding; that you may walk worthy of the Lord, fully pleasing Him, being fruitful in every good work and increasing in the knowledge of God.[16]

You remember how our brother, the prophet Daniel, while pleading for the forgiveness of the sins of all Israel, was met by the angel Gabriel who had come to give the aged saint skill to understand. The angel declared that Daniel was greatly beloved. My little children, you too are greatly beloved of heaven. Therefore consider the matter, and understand the vision that was given that day, over five hundred years before the birth of the Messiah.[17]

The words of the angel to

9 Luke 3:19-20
10 Mark 1:14, 15
11 Galatians 4:4
12 Genesis 3:15
13 II Peter 3:16
14 Daniel 12:10

15 Psalm 111:10
16 Colossians 1:9, 10
17 Daniel 9:22, 23

Daniel as he sat as a captive in literal Babylon, and to us who live in the time of the spiritual Babylon the Great,[18] are:

Seventy weeks are determined for your people and for your holy city, to finish the transgression, to make an end of sins, to make reconciliation for iniquity, to bring in everlasting righteousness, to seal up vision and prophecy, and to anoint the Most Holy.

Know therefore and understand, that from the going forth of the command to restore and build Jerusalem until Messiah the Prince, there shall be seven weeks and sixty-two weeks; the street shall be built again, and the wall, even in troublesome times. And after the sixty-two weeks Messiah shall be cut off, but not for Himself; and the people of the prince who is to come shall destroy the city and the sanctuary. The end of it shall be with a flood, and till the end of the war desolations are determined.

Then he shall confirm a covenant with many for one week; but in the middle of the week He shall bring an end to sacrifice and offering.[19]

God was cutting off a certain time for the literal nation of Israel to turn their hearts in sincerity to Him, to bring forth fruits worthy of their calling as His chosen nation. Then the Anointed One would appear. After that time, the literal nation of Israel would be cut off, even as they had cut off the Messiah, and the fellowship in the gospel would be extended to all those who would live by faith.[20] This was the time that was fulfilled. It was because of the fulfillment of this time that John the Baptist, Jesus Christ, the Apostles, and the disciples of all ages since that time have been declaring that the kingdom of heaven is at hand.[21]

When we speak of time on a normal calendar basis, seventy weeks is not a long time, just a few months more than a year. However, in this instance

---

18 Revelation 17:5

19 Daniel 9:24-27
20 Hab. 2:4; Rom. 1:17; Gal. 3:11;
   Heb. 10:38
21 Matt. 3:2, 4:17, 10:7; Mark 1:15

we are not talking about normal time, but prophetic time. Daniel wrote about the prophecy given to him by the angel Gabriel. According to the Bible, when referring to prophecy, time may be treated differently than in normal circumstances. This applies only to prophetic periods.

Consider the declaration God spoke when the Israelites spied out the land for forty days, and then decided that they could not trust God to give them victory and entrance into the land of Canaan. The Israelites were then cut off from the Promised Land a day for a year.[22] God decreed that they would spend a period of forty years wandering in the Wilderness of Sin in response to their rebellion against His command. They searched out the land for forty days; they would wander outside its border for forty years.

Likewise, when our brother Ezekiel was told to endure the prophetic judgments of God for the nations of Israel and Judah, he was instructed to lie on his side, a day for a year,[23] that his life might be an object lesson for the people of God. In both of these examples, God is very clear about this principle, because He reiterates His command twice in each case: a day for a year, a day for a year. The Bible reveals that a prophetic day is to be understood as a year of literal time.

You that are known of the Lord, know for certain that the mystery described to our brother Daniel, once understood, will greatly strengthen your confidence in the Word of God. Let us therefore apply this principle to the prophecy given to Daniel by the angel to determine when God predicted His Son would be anointed and cut off.

Earlier we read that the beginning of this period starts, from the going forth of the command to restore and build Jerusalem until Messiah the Prince.[24] This vision occurred around 538 B.C. while Daniel

---

22 Numbers 14:33, 34

23 Ezekiel 4:6
24 Daniel 9:25

was a captive in Babylon. God had promised that, although the Israelites were taken as prisoners of war to Babylon because of their infidelity to His commandments and their spiritual waywardness, God would be merciful and deliver them after they suffered for seventy years as slaves.[25] Our brother Daniel, being a student of the Scriptures even as you are my brethren, knew that the time was soon to be fulfilled. God had planned in love for the release of His children from literal bondage, even as He has planned in love for our freedom from spiritual captivity.

God raised up rulers, calling one of them by name long before he was born, so that they would comply with His plan to set His children free.[26] The angel revealed that there would be a command to restore and rebuild Jerusalem to her former condition, and the Bible reveals that such a command was issued by King Artaxerxes.[27] Under the leadership of our brother, the wise sage Ezra, a group of the children of Israel who were still remaining in Babylon under their new rulers, the Persians, departed for Jerusalem, arriving in the fall (September/October) of the year 457 B.C.[28] This decree marks the time when the nation of Israel was allowed to again practice her legal and spiritual rites. This also marks the beginning of the time period that was cut off for the fulfillment of the promises of the first coming of the Messiah.

We know that the seventy weeks of years [prophetic time] began in the fall of 457 B.C. Who is wise and understanding among you?[29] He who has wisdom will be able to understand this mystery. Remember, my beloved, prove all things,[30] for many deceivers are entered into the world.[31] Also from among yourselves men will rise up, speaking perverse things, to draw away disciples after themselves. Therefore watch, and remember… I did not cease to warn everyone.[32]

---

25 Jeremiah 25:11, 12, 29:10
26 Isaiah 44:28-45:1;
    II Chron. 36:22, 23
27 Ezra 7:11-26

28 Ezra 7:8
29 James 3:13
30 I Thessalonians 5:21
31 II John 1:7
32 Acts 20:30, 31

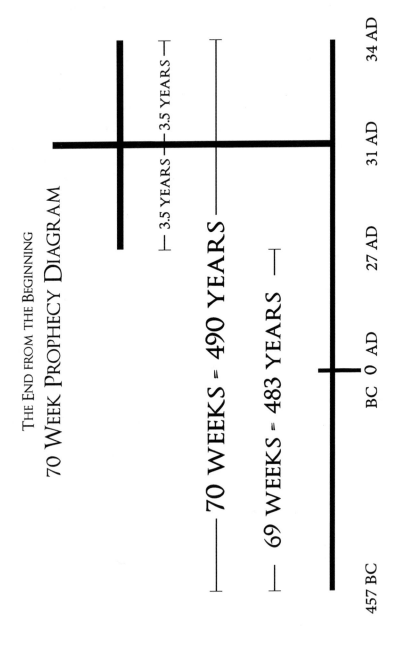

The End from the Beginning

70 Week Prophecy Diagram

70 WEEKS = 490 YEARS

69 WEEKS = 483 YEARS

3.5 YEARS — 3.5 YEARS

457 BC   BC 0 AD   27 AD   31 AD   34 AD

The figuring out of this seventy weeks of prophetic time involves calculating the time from the beginning of the prophecy until its completion, and also comprehending the meaning of the events foretold. Beloved, let us work together to understand this mystery.

Each week has seven days. Seventy weeks would have four hundred ninety days [70 weeks times 7 days]. According to the principle discovered in the Bible, in prophecy a day is equal to a year. So the entire period covered under this seventy week prophecy is four hundred ninety years.

The prophecy also states that until Messiah the Prince there shall be seven weeks and sixty-two weeks.[33] To make it easier to calculate, we will add these two figures together here, equaling sixty-nine weeks [7 plus 62]. We realize that in sixty-nine weeks there are 483 days [69 weeks multiplied by 7 days a week]. Since days are equal to years in prophecy, the time from the beginning of the prophecy until the appearance of the Messiah is 483 years.

We have one more calculation to perform, and then we will apply these numbers to the events of the prophecy and discover that God does indeed know the end from the beginning.

The final words of the prophecy include this prediction: Then he shall confirm a covenant with many for one week; but in the middle of the week He shall bring an end to sacrifice and offering.[34] Since one week has seven days, and in prophecy these days represent seven years, something taking place in the middle of the week means that it happens after three and a half days, which in prophecy means after 3½ literal years.

Dear chosen people of God, as we apply these figures to the events of this prophecy, we will see without a doubt that Jesus Christ is the Messiah. He who has ears let him hear![35]

The period of time for this prophecy began in the fall of 457 B.C. when the people of God were told to come out of Babylon, repair the temple of God, restore the law of God, and prepare for the

---

33 *Daniel 9:25*

34 *Daniel 9:27*
35 *Revelation 13:9*

coming of God in the flesh, Jesus the Messiah.[36] The angel told Daniel that the Messiah would appear exactly sixty-nine prophetic weeks later. We saw that this period of 69 weeks is 483 years. This means that, according to Bible prophecy, 483 years after 457 B.C., the Messiah would appear.

We subtract 457 B.C. from 483 years until the Messiah, and we get A.D. 26. Between the time B.C. (Before Christ) and the time A.D. (Anno Domini, which is Latin for, the year of our Lord), there is no year 0. Therefore, we have to add one year to this total because the change from B.C. to A.D does not include the use of a year 0 (zero). Therefore, the time for the fulfillment of this prediction is A.D. 27.

The Word predicts that God would come in the flesh and reveal Himself in the fall of A.D. 27. In that same year, we read that John the Baptist came to the River Jordan preaching a baptism of repentance, announcing that all should prepare the way of the Lord, for the salvation of God was soon to be revealed.[37] And it came to pass in those days that Jesus came from Nazareth of Galilee, and was baptized by John in the Jordan. And immediately, coming up from the water, He saw the heavens parting and the Spirit descending upon Him like a dove. Then a voice came from heaven, You are My beloved Son, in whom I am well pleased.[38]

So it was in the fall of A.D. 27, just as God had foretold through the angel Gabriel to the prophet Daniel more than five hundred years earlier, that this vision was sealed up, prophecy was fulfilled, and the Most Holy – the Son of God, Christ Jesus – was Anointed at His baptism.

God anointed Jesus of Nazareth

36 Ezra 7:8, 11-26

37 Luke 3:1-3
38 Mark 1:9-11

with the Holy Ghost and with power: He went about doing good, and healing all that were oppressed of the devil; for God was with him.[39] Over the course of the next three and a half years Christ healed many sick,[40] gave sight to the blind,[41] cleansed the lepers,[42] made the lame to walk, caused the deaf to hear, raised the dead back to life, and preached the gospel to the poor.[43] O, what a blessing it would have been there to witness the compassion of our Savior when He was in the flesh!

During this time, just as had been prophesied, the covenant made to the literal nation of Israel was confirmed.[44] Unfortunately, most of the children of Israel in the time of Christ responded just as their fathers had done when confronted by the prophets throughout her history:[45] they sought to kill Him who promised to be their Savior.[46]

The prophecy unveiled to Daniel by the angel Gabriel predicted that, in the middle of the week He shall bring an end to sacrifice and offering.[47] In the midst of the final week of probation that the nation of Israel was given to bring in righteousness, they took the Son of God, Jesus Christ, the Messiah, outside the walls of Jerusalem and hung Him on a tree. This happened exactly as foretold, three and a half years following His anointing in the fall of 27 A.D., at the time of the sacrifice of the Passover lamb in the spring of 31 A.D. When Jesus breathed His last on that dark afternoon, crying out, It is finished![48] the veil in the temple in the Holy Place was torn into two pieces, shredded from top to bottom.[49] The sacrificial system ended with the death of the Lamb of God, Christ Jesus, who takes away the sin of the world.[50] Jesus knew exactly when He was to be anointed the Christ; He knew what His ministry would be;[51] He knew

39 Acts 10:38
40 Luke 4:40
41 Luke 7:21
42 Mark 1:40-42
43 Luke 7:22
44 Daniel 9:27; Luke 1:72
45 Matthew 23:30, 32
46 Luke 11:47-54

47 Daniel 9:27
48 John 19:30
49 Matthew 27:51; Mark 15:38
50 John 1:29
51 Isaiah 61:1, 2; Luke 4:1, 2

exactly when He would lay
down His life.

Long before He was led up
Calvary where He asked
His Father to forgive His
tormentors,[52] Jesus knew how
much time was allotted to
the literal children of Israel
as a nation. When one of His
disciples asked how many
times we should forgive those
who hurt us and sin against
us, Jesus responded by saying
seventy times seven.[53] God
had waited with patience for
His wayward children to finish
the transgression, to make
an end of sins, to make
reconciliation for iniquity,
and to bring in everlasting
righteousness. He had cut
off 490 years – seventy times
seven –until He came to the
world to seal up vision and
prophecy, and to anoint the
Most Holy.

O dear friends in the faith,
when we see how clearly all
the elements of this prophecy
come together in the life of
Christ Jesus, we should praise
God together. Hallelujah!

---

52 Luke 23:34
53 Matthew 18:22

Chapter Five

THE INTERPRETATION IS SURE

John, a servant of God and a disciple of Jesus Christ, according to the faith of God's elect and the acknowledgment of the truth which accords with godliness, in hope of eternal life which God, who cannot lie, promised before time began;[1] to the remnant of believers who continue to contend for the faith that was once delivered to the saints:[2] Grace, mercy, and peace from God the Father and the Lord Jesus Christ our Savior.

We have seen and do know that the kingdom of God is not of this world.[3] Jesus knew before the foundation of the world what would happen to Him when He appeared in the flesh on this sin ravaged planet. He knew that when the infinite holiness of God is revealed in all its glory, sinful beings cannot bear to be in His presence, and so He veiled His majesty in the lowly garb of humanity.[4] Under the inspiration of Satan, the fallen creatures of earth put to death their heavenly Creator.

God knew from the beginning of time what would be the result of creating this world. He also knows the end of the spiritual conflict that rages in the heart of every man.

The prince of this world,[5] Satan, is as a roaring lion, seeking whom he may devour.[6] Therefore, beloved, do not think it strange concerning the fiery trial which is to try you, as though some strange thing happened to you; but rejoice to the extent that you partake of Christ's sufferings, that when His glory is revealed, you may also be glad with exceeding joy.[7]

I write now to you, because

---

1 *Titus 1:2,3*
2 *Jude 1:3*
3 *John 18:36*

4 *I Timothy 6:16; John 18:6*
5 *John 12:31*
6 *I Peter 5:8*
7 *I Peter 4:12, 13*

you are strong, and the word of God abides in you, and you have overcome the wicked one.[8] Yet you must understand that, although the kingdom of God is not of this world, the enemy of God and man has sought to establish his kingdom on this earth. I write to you who have known Him who is from the beginning[9] concerning the kingdoms of this world. You have heard of the many difficulties that the people of God encountered throughout history, being persecuted, stoned, sawn asunder, and wandering about as vagabonds.[10] Yet they were more than conquerors through Him who loves both them and us.[11] Even so now do we face such trials.

Therefore, my brethren united under the tear-stained banner of the cross: Fear not![12] Although it may at times seem as if the kingdoms of this world have defeated the people of God, remember that the greatness of the kingdoms under the whole heaven shall be given to the people, the saints of the Most High. His kingdom is an everlasting kingdom.[13]

God intended for our forefathers in the faith, the literal children of Israel, to be a praise in all the earth, and that through them a knowledge of God might be known throughout the earth.[14] But it was not to be. The Israelites did not want God to rule over them; instead, they desired to be like the nations around them.[15] They wanted to have a man rule them and not God. Our heavenly Father anticipated this sad development,[16] knowing that humanity often chooses to disregard the mercy of God and accept the tyranny of man in His place. Such is the history of man. Yet God demonstrates His love to us in that, while the kingdoms of Satan have held sway on the earth, our compassionate Father in heaven reveals to us that ultimately He is in control.

The Israelites rejected God and chose a man as their king. Led by sinful man, within a

8 I John 2:14
9 I John 2:13
10 Hebrews 11:35-40
11 Romans 8:37
12 Matthew 28:5

13 Daniel 7:27
14 Genesis 12:1-3
15 I Samuel 8:5-7
16 Deuteronomy 17:14

few generations the twelve tribes that were born of Jacob split into two kingdoms. The ten tribes called Israel lived in the north, and the tribes of Judah and Benjamin [the Jews] dwelt in the south of the Promised Land.

Although at times God raised up a ruler who was a man after His own heart,[17] most of the time these kingdoms suffered through numerous rulers who pursued their own selfish desires. The last monarch of the united kingdom, Solomon, although at one time reputed to be the wisest man alive,[18] became a fool because of his idolatry, immorality and greed. His foolishness led him into idolatrous rebellion against God, and he led the entire nation down into spiritual darkness.[19] Subsequently, the nation split into two, the northern tribes known as Israel and the southern tribes known as the Jews.

Very quickly the ten tribes in the north descended into open idolatry. These northern tribes rejected the God of heaven and began worshiping golden idols of cows.[20] As a consequence, God allowed them to be defeated by the armies of Assyria and taken away as prisoners of war. Never again are the people of the northern kingdom heard of in history.

Many times God sent prophets and messengers to warn His people, but they chose not to listen.[21] God had to discipline His people in love[22] because they were causing His character and His name to be blasphemed before the surrounding nations. Consequently, God allowed the forces of the king of Babylon to invade the land of the Jews and capture their capital, Jerusalem.[23]

Dear beloved, keep this in mind: God promised to send a Savior to rescue us from sin and the grave,[24] and He declared that His Son would come from the tribe of Judah.[25] God had to mercifully discipline His children while

---

17 I Samuel 13:14; Acts 13:22
18 I Kings 10:23, 24
19 I Kings 11:4-10;
    Deuteronomy 17:17

20 I Kings 12:28
21 II Chronicles 36:15, 16
22 Hebrews 12:6
23 II Chronicles 36:17-20
24 Genesis 3:15
25 Genesis 49:10

also making provision to fulfill His promises.

The armies of Babylon, led by king Nebuchadnezzar, attacked the Jewish kingdom and destroyed Jerusalem and its temple. In the process, Nebuchadnezzar took some of the leading youth of the royal family, castrated them,[26] and brought them to his court for training. Among those brought as prisoners of war and singled out for education in the schools of Babylon were our brothers Daniel, Hananiah, Azariah, and Mishael.

Daniel and the others were given three years of training in the schools of Babylon.[27] At the completion of their education they were found to be ten times wiser than the others because they remained faithful to the God of heaven.[28] God also gave Daniel the gift of understanding visions and dreams.[29] God revealed much of the end from the beginning through His consecrated servant Daniel.

O my dear brethren, called of God and chosen in the faith, how marvelous it is that when Satan seeks to destroy, God takes the curse and turns it into a blessing.[30] The defeat of the Israelites and the presence of Daniel and the other Jews in Babylon, while at the time a terrible tragedy, were foreseen by God. He used their calamities to give hope and courage to those of us who are living at the end of time and battling with the forces of spiritual Babylon.

Shortly after Daniel and his companions completed their training, King Nebuchadnezzar was given a most striking dream. This dream troubled him deeply, but he could not remember what he had seen in his night vision. He called together all his religious counselors, the magicians, the sorcerers, and the astrologers to tell him the dream and its interpretation. None of these so-called wise men were able to tell the dream, nor its interpretation, so the king rashly ordered them all to be slain.[31]

O my dear brethren, called of God is in control of all things,

---

26 II Kings 20:18; Isaiah 39:7
27 Daniel 1:5
28 Daniel 1:20
29 Daniel 1:17

30 Deuteronomy 23:5
31 Daniel 2:1-13

THE INTERPRETATION IS SURE

and He can cause all things to happen; all things except one. Even God cannot cause a person to turn from his wicked ways and accept His free offer of salvation. Only the individual can make that decision. God reveals to every soul the abundant evidence of His love, the truth of His ways, and the foolishness of sin. However God cannot and will not ever force someone to put his trust in Him against his own conscience. Each must make his own choice. [32] So it was for King Nebuchadnezzar; so it is for each of us.

Daniel was told of the decree of the king to execute all the counselors in Babylon, which included him and his three faithful compatriots. Daniel went to the king of Babylon and politely sought a temporary reprieve from his order so that he could learn the dream. When this was granted, Daniel quickly assembled his friends and they met together with the King of the Universe for earnest prayer. [33] The God of heaven honored their prayers, and

Daniel was shown the dream of king Nebuchadnezzar and its interpretation in a night vision. You can imagine how they rejoiced together at the mercy of God, [34] even as we also ought to praise Him, for His mercy endures forever. [35]

Daniel went in before the king, and taking no personal credit for the matter, told the king that God had revealed the dream. [36] This is the dream that God gave to Nebuchadnezzar, and its interpretation:

Behold, a great image! This great image, whose splendor was excellent, stood before you [Nebuchadnezzar]; and its form was awesome. This image's head was of fine gold, its chest and arms of silver, its belly and thighs of bronze, its legs of iron, its feet partly of iron and partly of clay.

You watched while a stone was cut out without hands, which struck the image on its feet of iron and clay, and broke them in pieces. Then the iron, the clay, the bronze, the silver, and

---

32 Isaiah 1:18
33 Daniel 2:16-18; Matthew 18:20

34 Daniel 2:20-23
35 Psalm 136:1; I Chron. 16:34
36 Daniel 2:27, 28

the gold were crushed together, and became like chaff from the summer threshing floors; the wind carried them away so that no trace of them was found. And the stone that struck the image became a great mountain and filled the whole earth.

This is the dream. Now we will tell the interpretation of it before the king.

You, O king [Nebuchadnezzar], are a king of kings. For the God of heaven has given you a kingdom, power, strength, and glory; and wherever the children of men dwell, or the beasts of the field and the birds of the heaven, He has given them into your hand, and has made you ruler over them all - you are this head of gold.

But after you shall arise another kingdom inferior to yours; then another, a third kingdom of bronze, which shall rule over all the earth. And the fourth kingdom shall be as strong as iron, inasmuch as iron breaks in pieces and shatters everything; and like iron that crushes, that kingdom will break in pieces and crush all the others. Whereas you saw the feet and toes, partly of potter's clay and partly of iron, the kingdom shall be divided; yet the strength of the iron shall be in it, just as you saw the iron mixed with ceramic clay. And as the toes of the feet were partly of iron and partly of clay, so the kingdom shall be partly strong and partly fragile. As you saw iron mixed with ceramic clay, they will mingle with the seed of men; but they will not adhere to one another, just as iron does not mix with clay.

And in the days of these kings the God of heaven will set up a kingdom which shall never be destroyed; and the kingdom shall not be left to other people; it shall break in pieces and consume all these kingdoms, and it shall stand forever. Inasmuch as you saw that the stone was cut out of the mountain without hands, and that it broke in pieces the iron, the bronze, the clay, the silver, and the gold - the great God has made known to the king what will come to pass after this. The dream is certain, and its interpretation is sure.[37]

---

37 Daniel 2:31-45

Beloved, God arranged circumstances concerning this dream so that He would receive honor and glory, and the foolishness of all false religions would be proven vain and useless. The king of Babylon and his people – indeed, almost all nations - worship things that they make for themselves. In the time of Nebuchadnezzar, the people bowed before literal idols of gold and silver. In our time, while these idols still exist, in many cultures people carry their "gods" of gold and silver in their pockets. Moreover, in contemporary society people pay homage to the gods of television, music, sports, philosophy, power, business, money, bank accounts, computers, and education.

God wants all peoples in the world to understand that He is God and there is no other.[38] Those who make idols or worship them are just like their objects of worship: they have eyes but cannot see; they have mouths but they cannot speak; ears they have but they cannot hear.[39] How pitiful it is that men believe they can make their own god, when all the while their

Creator is seeking to draw them with His love.

In the dream God gave to Nebuchadnezzar He revealed that there would be a succession of kingdoms that would arise, beginning with the head of gold, Babylon, and continuing down into the feet of iron and clay mixed together. Beloved, God would not have us be ignorant concerning these things.[40] I briefly write to you the history of these kingdoms as God unveiled them in the time of Daniel, more than five hundred years before the birth of Jesus.

King Nebuchadnezzar reigned over one of the most glorious of kingdoms the world has ever known. Centered in the city of Babylon on the Euphrates River, his dominion spread to Egypt and the Mediterranean in the West, and beyond the Persian Gulf in the east. His throne was set in a city thought to be impregnable. Babylon was the virtual ruler of the world from 606 through 538 B.C. But alas, God declared that Babylon was to fall, and fall it did.

38 Isaiah 44:6
39 Psalm 115:5-8; 135:16-18
40 I Thessalonians 4:13

43

The Bible is very plain about the next kingdom to succeed the reign of Babylon. In the dream given of God, the idol is adorned with a chest and arms of silver. As we proceed down the figure of the man, so too we descend in the quality of the metal represented. As silver is less valuable than gold, so the next kingdom was less magnificent in splendor than the rule of Babylon. God gives explicit details about the fall of Babylon, of which we will talk more later, and how it was conquered by the powers of the unified forces of the Medes and the Persians.[41] This silver kingdom reigned over the earth from the time it deposed Babylon in 539 B.C., until it was conquered in 331 B.C.

The next metal of the idol was bronze, and again the Bible identifies the next world superpower as Greece.[42] Under the leadership of Alexander the Great, the armies of Greece swept across the land, gaining victories in every territory they opposed. It is said that Alexander never lost a war.

However, he lost the most important battle of them all: with himself. Alexander died a drunken young man, the victim of his own insatiable appetite and lack of self-control. No wonder it was the belly of the idol that was of bronze! The kingdom of Greece rapidly deteriorated into four smaller kingdoms following his death, and never again gained the luster and power it had under "the Great."

Looking down the body of the Metal Man we find that the legs are of iron. The next global power to extend its military and economic might across the landscape of world history was the iron monarchy of Rome. The authority of Rome spread far and wide, from Europe into Egypt, from Babylon into Persia. It was the Roman Empire that vanquished the Greek civilization, at least in military dominance, and it was the Romans that were to play a role in the fulfillment of the prophecies concerning our blessed Savior Jesus Christ.[43]

---

41 Daniel 5:30, 31
42 Daniel 8:21

43 Luke 2:1-7; 3:1-4, 21, 22;
   23:1-3, 20-24

It was during the rule of Rome that what was written came to pass: For unto us a Child is born, unto us a Son is given; and the government will be upon His shoulder. And His name will be called Wonderful, Counselor, Mighty God, Everlasting Father, Prince of Peace. Of the increase of His government and peace there will be no end, upon the throne of David and over His kingdom, to order it and establish it with judgment and justice from that time forward, even forever. The zeal of the Lord of hosts will perform this.[44] When the Son of God became the curse of sin for us,[45] it was under the cruel iron rule of Rome.

Each of these kingdoms came and went, exactly as God predicted. Blessed be the name of God forever and ever, for wisdom and might are His. And He changes the times and the seasons; He removes kings and raises up kings; He gives wisdom to the wise and knowledge to those who have understanding. He reveals deep and secret things; He knows

what is in the darkness, and light dwells with Him.[46]

O dear elect in the faith, those who refuse to bow before any object of false worship, each of these kingdoms is represented as a piece of an idol because each tried to seduce, coerce, and demand that the people of God participate in false worship. Each had rulers who claimed to be a god, and threatened and caused that as many as would not worship their images to be killed.[47]

King Nebuchadnezzar, in defiance of the dream given him of God, set up an idol to himself made entirely out of gold and demanded all to bow before his image.[48] King Darius of Medo-Persia passed a law prohibiting the worship of any other being except him upon pain of death.[49] Alexander the Great, in a fury of drunken stupor, declared himself a god. The Roman emperors required that all bow at the feet of the Caesars and acknowledge their divinity, upon penalty of being

44 Isaiah 9:6, 7; Luke 1:32, 33
45 Galatians 3:13

46 Daniel 2:20-22
47 Revelation 13:15
48 Daniel 3:4-6
49 Daniel 6:6-9

thrown to the lions or some other cruel death.[50]

These kingdoms were raised up by Satan, yet were permitted by God who sees the end from the beginning. We shall learn that this great wickedness did not end with these rulers, but their diabolical madness was exceeded by the vice-regent of the prince of darkness himself. In each case, the power of the government joined forces with the idolatrous religious power prevailing in the empire to enforce false worship, usually for financial purposes. Satan worked through these united powers – the government and the religion – to try to exterminate the people of God. As it was in the past, so it shall be in the future.

O how grateful we can be that the dream of the Metal Man did not end in the toes of the idol, and of religious rulers uniting with governments to destroy the people of God. My dear friends, the dream is certain, and its interpretation is sure. Soon, very soon, the God of heaven will set up a kingdom which shall never be destroyed; and the kingdom shall not be left to other people; it shall break in pieces and consume all these kingdoms, and it shall stand forever. The stone that was cut out of the mountain without hands shall break in pieces the iron, the bronze, the clay, the silver, and the gold.[51] His dominion is an everlasting dominion, which shall not pass away, and His kingdom the one which shall not be destroyed.[52] The great God has made known to us what will come to pass. Hallelujah!

Beloved, you recall that we are to test all things; hold fast what is good. Do not despise prophecies. Do not quench the Spirit.[53] Even so now, I counsel you to verify all that I have written to you. I have not written to you because you do not know the truth, but because you know it, and that no lie is of the truth.[54] We are of God. He who knows God hears us; he who is not of God does not hear us. By this we know

50 Hebrews 11:35-40

51 Daniel 2:45, 44
52 Daniel 7:14
53 I Thessalonians 5:21, 20, 19
54 I John 2:21

the spirit of truth and the spirit of error.[55]

It is written that in the mouth of two or three witnesses shall every word be established.[56] God graciously provided another witness for us that will confirm the testimony that I shared with you concerning the kingdoms of the world.

Our brother Daniel, yet a captive in Babylon, was later given a vision that reinforced the dream that God had given to Nebuchadnezzar concerning the kingdoms of this world. Daniel described the scene as following:

Behold, the four winds of heaven were stirring up the Great Sea. And four great beasts came up from the sea, each different from the other. The first was like a lion, and had eagle's wings. I watched till its wings were plucked off; and it was lifted up from the earth and made to stand on two feet like a man, and a man's heart was given to it.

And suddenly another beast, a second, like a bear. It was raised up on one side, and had three ribs in its mouth between its teeth. And they said thus to it: 'Arise, devour much flesh!'

After this I looked, and there was another, like a leopard, which had on its back four wings of a bird. The beast also had four heads, and dominion was given to it.

After this I saw in the night visions, and behold, a fourth beast, dreadful and terrible, exceedingly strong. It had huge iron teeth; it was devouring, breaking in pieces, and trampling the residue with its feet. It was different from all the beasts that were before it, and it had ten horns.

I was considering the horns, and there was another horn, a little one, coming up among them, before whom three of the first horns were plucked out by the roots. And there, in this horn, were eyes like the eyes of a man, and a mouth speaking pompous words.

55 I John 4:6
56 Deut. 17:6, 19:15; Matt. 18:16; II Cor. 13:1

I watched till thrones were put in place, and the Ancient of Days was seated; His garment was white as snow, and the hair of His head was like pure wool. His throne was a fiery flame, its wheels a burning fire; a fiery stream issued and came forth from before Him. A thousand thousands ministered to Him; ten thousand times ten thousand stood before Him. The court was seated, and the books were opened.

I watched then because of the sound of the pompous words which the horn was speaking; I watched till the beast was slain, and its body destroyed and given to the burning flame. As for the rest of the beasts, they had their dominion taken away, yet their lives were prolonged for a season and a time.

I was watching in the night visions, and behold, One like the Son of Man, coming with the clouds of heaven! He came to the Ancient of Days, and they brought Him near before Him. Then to Him was given dominion and glory and a kingdom, that all peoples, nations, and languages should serve Him. His dominion is an everlasting dominion, which shall not pass away, and His kingdom the one which shall not be destroyed.[57]

Beloved, here again we see a vision, given by God to man, that we his servants might know the things that must shortly come to pass.[58] As Daniel looked on these scenes, he was troubled by what he saw.[59] He was even more disturbed when he was told the significance of the beasts he saw in vision.[60]

Those great beasts, which are four, are four kings which arise out of the earth. But the saints of the Most High shall receive the kingdom, and possess the kingdom forever, even forever and ever.[61]

Four great beasts; four great kingdoms. There were four world empires described in the dream of the Metal Man. There are four global superpowers

---

57 *Daniel 7:2-14*
58 *Revelation 1:1*
59 *Daniel 7:15*
60 *Daniel 7:28*
61 *Daniel 7:17, 18*

throughout history given in this vision. Daniel understood this much.

The first beast, like a lion having its wings plucked off, represents the kingdom of Babylon. Having to stand upon his feet like a man, and being given the heart of man, is symbolic of the experience of Nebuchadnezzar when he finally gave his heart and life to God.[62]

The second beast, like a bear raised up on one side, parallels the kingdom of Medo-Persia. The Medes rose first in power, but when the Persians came up, they rose up higher. The three ribs are symbolic of the three territories that this empire conquered.

Following the rule of Medo-Persians, another world empire rushed across the page of history. Like a leopard flying swiftly across the landscape of time, Alexander the Great and his armies swept away all those that opposed his forces. Alexander, however, could not conquer his own passions, and his dominion was divided, like the four heads of the beast, among four of his generals.

The Bible is very clear about the fourth beast. It depicts a fourth kingdom on earth after the fall of Greece, which shall be different from all other kingdoms, and shall devour the whole earth, trample it and break it in pieces. This kingdom is exceedingly dreadful, with its teeth of iron and its nails of bronze, which devoured, broke in pieces, and trampled the residue with its feet.[63] This is a very accurate description of the Roman Empire which destroyed all countries that did not agree to its terms of conquest.

Regarding the ten horns that were on the head of this dreadful beast, remember that there were ten toes on the idol that God displayed in the earlier dream given to Nebuchadnezzar. Out of the Roman Empire arose ten kingdoms. Most of the major nations [kingdoms] of modern Europe are direct descendants

---

62 *Daniel 4:34-37*

63 *Daniel 7:19*

of these ten toe powers. For centuries these toes tried to unite in various alliances, both political and marital, but they did not and will not adhere to one another, just as iron does not mix with clay.[64] History has verified the truth of the Word of God.

Beloved, there is one more power which we need to be aware of, and this power is far more hideous, far more deceptive than any of the preceding kingdoms. It is the little horn power which came up out from the midst of the horns of the fourth beast, before which three of the other horns fell. This power speaks pompous words against the Most High, persecutes the saints of the Most High, and intends to change times and law.[65] This horrendous creature was organized and formed for the advancement of the powers of darkness. It is to the masterpiece of deception formed by Satan that we will next turn our attention.

Fellow believers, I charge you before God and the Lord Jesus Christ, who will judge the living and the dead at His appearing and His kingdom:[66] be faithful unto death and you will be given the crown of life.[67]

Pray, deeply loved in the Lord. Pray.

---

64 *Daniel 2:43*
65 *Daniel 7:25*
66 *II Timothy 4:1*
67 *Revelation 2:10*

Chapter Six

THE DRAGON, THE BEAST, AND THE FALSE PROPHET

John, a servant of God and a disciple of the Lord Jesus Christ, to the twelve tribes which are scattered abroad: Greetings.

My brethren, count it all joy when you fall into various trials, knowing that the testing of your faith produces patience. But let patience have its perfect work, that you may be perfect and complete, lacking nothing.

If any of you lacks wisdom, let him ask of God, who gives to all liberally and without reproach, and it will be given to him.[1] I exhort you to ask for wisdom from God as we share together.

Hear, O Israel: The Lord our God, the Lord is one! You shall love the Lord your God with all your heart, with all your soul, and with all your strength.[2] We are called to love God with our entire being. He is one. Yet the Scripture reveals a mystery: a unity among God as One yet having different personalities.

In the beginning God created the heavens and the earth.[3] In the beginning was the Word, and the Word was with God, and the Word was God. He was in the beginning with God. All things were made through Him, and without Him nothing was made that was made.[4] God spoke the Word[5] while the Spirit was moving on the face of the deep[6] and creation took place. When God was to perform His crowning act of creation in making man, He spoke, Let Us make man in Our image, according to Our likeness.[7] God refers to Himself as Us, and that He made man in Our image. Both of these are plural.

In a similar manner, Jesus commanded that we are to

---

1 *James 1:2-5*
2 *Deuteronomy 6:4, 5*

3 *Genesis 1:1*
4 *John 1:1-3*
5 *Genesis 1:3, 6, 9, 11, 14, 20, 24*
6 *Genesis 1:2*
7 *Genesis 1:27*

go and make disciples of all the nations, baptizing them in the name of the Father and of the Son and of the Holy Spirit.[8] There are three persons involved here, but there is only one name. Scriptures declare that there are three that bear witness in heaven: the Father, the Word, and the Holy Spirit; and these three are one.[9] Several times Jesus tried to teach us that He and His Father are One, [10] even as the Holy Spirit is also One with Them.[11]

The Holy Bible makes it clear that there is only one God, and that He manifests Himself as three unique persons: the Father, the Son, and the Holy Spirit. This is indeed a mystery. In marriage it is a mystery how two can become one flesh;[12] yet those who have been joined together through many a year can testify to the truth of their unity.

Beloved, I seek to make known unto you the truth of God; I also seek to make known to you the snares of Satan. God gave His Word to deliver us; even so the devil crafted a fiendish plot to deceive us. You know that the mystery of lawlessness is already at work;[13] the extent of this iniquity is truly astounding.

I beseech you, elect according to the grace that is in Christ Jesus, study the Bible as if your life depends upon it;[14] plead for the Holy Spirit that you might be given the spirit of understanding; pray for angelic protection as you learn of this impostor government.

In the Word of God it is written that the Father, the Son, and the Holy Spirit have been One in heaven since before creation. The devil was in heaven[15] and he knows about the government of the kingdom of God. He has seen how God rules in truth, righteousness and judgment.

In his devious madness, Satan created a counterfeit to the kingdom of God. The satanic kingdom is a cleverly crafted parallel to the true kingdom, specifically designed to deceive.

8 Matthew 28:19
9 I John 5:7
10 John 10:30, 17:11, 21
11 John 14:16-21, 26; 15:26
12 Genesis 2:24; Ephesians 5:31
13 II Thessalonians 2:7
14 John 5:39, 40
15 Isaiah 14:12

Only those who test all things by the Holy Scriptures[16] and fortify their minds with the truths of the Word of God will be able to distinguish between the true and the counterfeit.

The Bible gives a brief description of this satanic trinity, referring to them as the dragon, the beast, and the false prophet.[17] God has much to say about this wicked system, and He shares it with us so that we will not be deceived. As our Lord Himself has said, so I tell you now again: take heed that no one deceives you.[18]

The symbol of the dragon is clearly described and identified in Scripture. The Word of God explains that there was in heaven a great, fiery red dragon having seven heads and ten horns, and seven diadems on his heads. And war broke out in heaven: Michael and his angels fought with the dragon; and the dragon and his angels fought, but they did not prevail, nor was a place found for them in heaven any longer. So the great dragon was cast out, that serpent of old, called the Devil and Satan, who deceives the whole world; he was cast to the earth, and his angels were cast out with him.[19]

The dragon is Satan, the devil, the old serpent who deceived Adam and Eve in the Garden of Eden long years ago. The rebellion by this fallen angel, formerly known as Lucifer [the Morning Star], now known as Satan [the Accuser], did not begin in the Garden, but in heaven itself, and so he along with his followers were cast out onto the earth.[20] He boasted while yet in heaven: 'I will ascend into heaven, I will exalt my throne above the stars of God; I will also sit on the mount of the congregation on the farthest sides of the north; I will ascend above the heights of the clouds, I will be like the Most High.'[21] The primary focus of the belief system of the devil, and all those who follow him, is I. His is a system of selfishness.

Lucifer, a covering cherub on

---

16 I John 4:1
17 Revelation 16:13
18 Matthew 24:4

19 Revelation 12:3, 7-9
20 Revelation 12:4
21 Isaiah 14:12-14

the throne of God, was a created being, and he was perfect when he was created.[22] However, because of the mystery of iniquity, in his pride he rebelled against the government of God and sought to set up his own dominion. He planned to place his throne above that of the Most High and the Savior.[23] Satan desired to become God, even the Most High, the Ancient of Days, God the Father.[24]

My brethren, do not fear, and do not be deceived. Our Lord Jesus Christ saw Satan fall from heaven,[25] and He shall crush this fallen angel once and for all very shortly.[26] We are not ignorant of the devices of the evil one.[27] When it suits his purpose, Satan appears like a serpent in the tree of the knowledge of good and evil in Eden claiming that man might be like God,[28] reflecting his desire to become God. At other times he transforms himself into an

angel of light,[29] leading souls into perdition because they love not the truth of the Word of God.[30]

Therefore we should not be surprised that he would want to be as God the Father. Satan is indeed a father. Jesus called him the father of lies, because he abode not in the truth, and there is no truth in him.[31]

Little children, I come to you speaking the truth in love.[32] Love that is not in truth is not love at all, but a subtle deception that appeals to our senses, even as the serpent appealed to the senses of Eve at the tree where she was deceived.[33] Remember that when Satan came to her, he did not immediately tell lies. First he appealed to her senses of sight and sound, for a beautiful, talking serpent was a remarkable thing to behold. Then the enemy quoted what God said, but manipulated the Word of God for his own purposes. The fallen angel cast

---

22 Ezekiel 28:14
23 Exodus 26:35; 25:24, 25;
    Revelation 4:5, 2
24 Daniel 7:9, 13
25 Luke 10:18
26 Romans 16:20
27 II Corinthians 2:11
28 Genesis 3:5

29 II Corinthians 11:14
30 II Thessalonians 2:10
31 John 8:44
32 Ephesians 4:15
33 Genesis 3:6

doubt on what God said as to whether He really meant it. As our first mother pondered the confusion that was placed in her mind, the devil spoke his first direct lie: you will not surely die.[34]

That which has been is what will be; that which is done is what will be done; there is nothing new under the sun.[35] The same tactics that Satan used against our forefathers in the beginning he will attempt against us in this last hour. He will not speak direct lies immediately, but he will mingle lies with the truth for the purpose of deceiving. He will cast doubt on the truth, will insinuate that the Bible cannot be trusted but that we should trust our senses, and he shall seek to cause the children of God to lose confidence in the Almighty. The most effective way for the devil to fulfill this dreadful task is to create a counterfeit of what God has done.

Elect of God, by grace through faith,[36] as the Word of God reveals this mystery to us, I counsel you to be of good courage. Although the powers of darkness have been allowed to work their schemes of treachery, God knew these plans before they came to pass, and He alone is in control. And so, dearly beloved, as we head into the final conflict with the forces of evil, be strong and of good courage![37] The God of heaven will prosper us,[38] and to those who remain faithful, entrance will be supplied abundantly into the everlasting kingdom of our Lord and Savior Jesus Christ.[39]

God revealed the truth about the father of lies, Satan, in the twelfth chapter of the book of Revelation. Immediately following the description of the devil and his work, we find the description given of the son of Satan. Not surprisingly, the son has a character like that of his father, Satan.

---

34 Genesis 3:4
35 Ecclesiastes 1:9

36 Ephesians 2:8
37 Joshua 1:9
38 Nehemiah 2:20
39 II Peter 1:11

John saw a beast rising up out of the sea, having seven heads and ten horns, and on his horns ten crowns, and on his heads a blasphemous name.[40] The Bible portrays Satan as a great, fiery red dragon having seven heads and ten horns, and seven diadems on his heads.[41] The son of Satan is a beast having heads and horns just like his father the dragon. Like father like son.

Now the beast which he saw was like a leopard, his feet were like the feet of a bear, and his mouth like the mouth of a lion.[42] Remember, beloved, that God revealed these same four beasts to our brother Daniel in a dream[43] (see chapter five). Remember also that these four beasts represent the governments that united with the religious powers of those nations, and Satan used these unholy alliances to persecute the people of God.

Notice beloved, that there is an important difference between the way Daniel describes the four beast kingdoms and the way they are shown to John. Daniel sees a lion, a bear, a leopard, and then a horrible beast. John describes the same four beasts in reverse order: a horrible beast, a leopard, a bear and a lion. The reason they are in opposite orders is because they are seen from different points in time. Daniel is looking into the future from the time of the Babylonian kingdom, represented as the lion. He then sees Medo-Persia, Greece, Rome, and the kingdoms that arise out of her. John is living in the time of the fourth beast, Rome, which is made up of a mixture of the beliefs of the three former powers, Greece, Medo-Persia, and Babylon, consecutively. The beast John describes is a conglomeration of the worst of all four worldwide empires, and is a work of demonic, deceptive genius.

The Bible tells that the dragon

---

40 *Revelation 13:1*
41 *Revelation 12:3*
42 *Revelation 13:2*
43 *Daniel 7:3-7*

gave this beast his power, his throne, and great authority.[44] It is here that we can begin to see the manner that the devil is seeking to counterfeit the work of God. Jesus said that He shares His throne with His Father,[45] and that He received His power[46] and authority from His Father in heaven.[47] So too, the false son receives his power, his throne, and great authority from his father, the devil.

The hope of our salvation is based on the blood of the Son of God shed on Calvary. Jesus received a death blow because of our iniquity,[48] but He rose again as conqueror over sin and the grave.[49] The devil tries to copy the death and resurrection of the Son of God by causing one of the heads of the son of Satan to appear as if it had been mortally wounded, and his deadly wound was healed.[50] Notice that this wound is only as if it had been mortally wounded, not that the beast actually died. Satan cannot cause the dead to come back to life, even as he cannot create life.

The Bible says that as a consequence of this deadly wound being healed, all the world marveled and followed the beast.[51] The son of Satan gained power, popularity and strength through its supposed death and resurrection. If anyone has an ear, let him hear;[52] be not deceived.[53] All who dwell on the earth will worship him, whose names have not been written in the Book of Life of the Lamb slain from the foundation of the world.[54]

When the Son of God was on earth, He was always directing people to worship His Father in heaven.[55] Jesus said that those who honored Him would also be honoring His Father.[56] As the Son of God Jesus accepted worship,[57] and those who share in His love worship God the Father.[58]

---

44 Revelation 13:2
45 Revelation 3:21
46 John 10:18
47 Matthew 28:18
48 Revelation 5:9
49 I Corinthians 15:20-24
50 Revelation 13:3

51 Revelation 13:3
52 Revelation 13:9
53 Luke 21:8
54 Revelation 13:8
55 John 4:23, 24
56 John 5:23
57 John 20:28, 29
58 II John 1:9

As it is with the true, so it is with the counterfeit. The Scriptures declare that whoever worships this beast, the son of Satan, actually worships the dragon, Satan, who gave authority to the beast; and they worshiped the beast.[59] However, there is a significant difference between the manner which the Son of God and the son of Satan cause people to worship their respective fathers. The difference is found in the character of the two eternal opposites.

Jesus Christ, as an obedient, humble Son, gave glory and honor to His Father through His life, His words, and His actions. The Son of God urged all to worship God the Father directly,[60] because the Father loves us.[61] The character of the Son of God is like that of His Father, and it was to reveal His character that He came into this world.[62]

The son of Satan, as a selfish, egotistical beast, does not want to attribute any glory or honor to his father. The son has the same character that actuates Satan, which we read is centered in self: 'I will ascend…, I will exalt…; I will sit…; I will ascend…, I will be like the Most High.'[63] Although he will not tell people to worship the devil directly, through his actions and character this devilish beast, the son of Satan, will cause people to worship his father, Satan. The son of Satan wants all the power and praise for himself because he is just like his father the devil.

As we read on in the description that God gives of this horrible counterfeit to the Son of God, we can be grateful that God forewarned us about this demonic creature, and we can give thanks that we do not have to be afraid because God also declares that this beast will come to an end and be destroyed. O what a marvelous God we serve. He knew the end of this son of Satan from the beginning, even before he was created in the wicked imagination of the devil.

---

59 Revelation 13:4
60 Matthew 4:10; John 4:23, 24
61 John 16:27
62 John 1:18; 5:37; 7:29

63 Isaiah 14:13, 14

God the Father anointed His Son, Jesus of Nazareth, with the Holy Spirit and with power, who went about doing good and healing all who were oppressed by the devil, for God was with Him.[64] From the time of His baptism in the fall of 27 A.D., until His crucifixion on the cruel cross of Calvary outside of Jerusalem[65] at Passover in 31 A.D., there elapsed a period of three and a half years.

In the vision given to Daniel by the angel Gabriel, it was foretold that the Messiah would be anointed, that He would confirm the covenant, and then in the middle of the week He would cause sacrifice and offering to cease[66] (see chapter four). We came to understand that these prophecies were fulfilled in the life of the Son of God. Jesus was baptized in the Jordan River and anointed by the Holy Spirit.[67] He preached the gospel to those who were broken hearted and longing to be free from sin.[68] On Passover He offered up His life as the Lamb of God at the Place of the Skull, and the veil in the temple was torn in two from top to bottom.[69]

God gives us warning that this beast, created by the father of lies, would be given authority to reign for forty-two months.[70] The Son of God proclaimed the kingdom of God on earth for a literal three and a half years. The son of Satan is permitted a corresponding *prophetic* period of time to demonstrate the principles of the kingdom of the prince of the power of the air,[71] Satan. Beloved, here again is another predictive mystery that God wants us to clearly understand.

Each year has twelve months. Three years is equal to thirty-six months, and adding another half a year [six months] gives us forty-two months. Therefore, the period forty-two months is the same as three and a half years.

Take this one step further. According to the Bible, each month has thirty days (not

---

64 *Acts 10:38*
65 *Hebrews 13:13*
66 *Daniel 9:24-27*
67 *John 1:32-33*
68 *Luke 4:18, 19*

69 *Mark 15:38*
70 *Revelation 13:5*
71 *Ephesians 2:2*

31, 29, or 28 as on our current calendar). Therefore, each year has three hundred and sixty days (12 months times 30 days a month). The period covering three and a half years covers a total of one thousand two hundred and sixty days (3 1/2 years times 360 days).

Finally, recall that when we were talking about the vision given to Daniel concerning how long it would be until the coming of the Son of God, we discovered a Biblical principle concerning time. When discussing prophetic periods of time, one day is equal to one year.[72] Let us apply this Biblical principle to the prophecy we are looking at now.

Jesus Christ, the Son of God, ministered in the flesh on this earth for a literal period of 3 ½ years. The Bible says that the son of Satan would set up his kingdom on earth for a period of prophetic 42 months, which by way of interpretation refers to a period of 1,260 years!

God wanted us to know of a certainty that this power would indeed be allowed to prevail and prosper in this world for this long period of time, and so He warned us about it many different ways. Twice God speaks directly of this period as 1,260 days.[73] Twice the Bible refers to this time as forty-two months.[74] On three separate occasions the Scriptures warn us about the long dominion of the son of Satan by indicating it will endure for a time, times, and a half a time.[75] Each of these times represents a prophetic year.[76] A time is one year, times is two years, and half a time means half a year. This totals three and a half prophetic times, the same as the period given in the other predictions.

Surely it is not a coincidence that when our brother the prophet Elijah prayed that it would not rain, God did not send His blessing for a literal 3 ½ years.[77] When the two witnesses prophesied clothed in sackcloth there was no rain for a prophetic 3 ½ years.[78] Just as

72 Numbers 14:33; Ezekiel 4:6

73 Revelation 11:3; 12:6
74 Revelation 11:2; 13:5
75 Daniel 7:25; 12:7; Revelation 12:14
76 Daniel 4:16, 32, 36
77 I Kings 17:1; 18:1; James 5:17
78 Revelation 11:3, 6

there was a literal period of no rain in the history of the nation of Israel, so too, there was a prophetic time of no rain when the souls of men thirsted for God but were not quenched during the Dark Ages. The literal and the prophetic periods occurred for the same reason: the people of God turned their backs on Him[79] and were worshipping idols.[80]

Fellow believers, when something is written once in the Word of God, we should heed what is written. When God believes that something is important enough to include it in His Word twice, we should surely take notice. But if, as in this time prophecy about the son of Satan, our heavenly Father is so concerned about this matter that He presents it seven different times, in three different ways in the Holy Scriptures, then we must pay attention to what He is seeking to reveal to us. He who has ears to hear, let him hear![81]

There is another important parallel that we need to notice between the Son of God and the son of Satan. While He was on earth, Jesus demonstrated in His life that He is indeed God. His miracles testified to His divinity.[82] His words told of His being One with the eternal God.[83] His power confirmed His claim to having the authority of God.[84] Jesus Christ is God.

The son of Satan, in his effort to impersonate the Son of God, claims to be God on earth. The son of Satan is revealed: he is the man of sin, the son of perdition, who opposes and exalts himself above all that is called God or that is worshiped, so that he sits as God in the temple of God, showing himself that he is God.[85]

Brethren, you recall that our Lord and Savior Jesus Christ was accused of being a blasphemer and a law-breaker by the fraudulent priests of His day. When Jesus forgave the sins of a man who was paralyzed, and then healed him, the phony prelates brought accusations

---

79 Ezekiel 8:16
80 I Kings 16:32, 33
81 Matthew 11:15

82 John 14:10, 11
83 John 8:58
84 Matt. 9:6; Mark 2:10; Luke 5:24
85 II Thessalonians 2:3, 4

against the Son of God for pardoning this man's sins.[86]

Another time Jesus healed a poor woman on the Sabbath. She had borne her infirmity many years. Instead of praising God that this dear woman was loosed from her illness, the self-righteous priests condemned the Son of God for transgressing the Sabbath.[87] Both of the charges brought by these hypocrites were false because Jesus is God. Therefore, His claims to divinity were not blasphemy, but godly truth.

Contrary to the truth spoken by the Son of God, the son of Satan was given a mouth speaking great things and blasphemies, and he opened his mouth in blasphemy against God, to blaspheme His name, His tabernacle, and those who dwell in heaven.[88] In seeking to counterfeit the Son of God, this blasphemous power claims to be divine, asserts that it can control the human conscience,

and makes the allegation that it has the ability to forgive sins. He blasphemes the name of God on earth by declaring that he represents the Creator of the Universe, when in fact he is the son of Satan. This beast blasphemes the tabernacle of God and those that dwell in heaven, because it is there that the Son of God is now ministering on our behalf[89] as our compassionate High Priest.

When the Son of God was on earth, He magnified the law of God. Jesus did not come to destroy the Law or the Prophets, but to fulfill them. Indeed, one jot or one tittle will by no means pass from the law till all is fulfilled,[90] for it is easier for heaven and earth to pass away than for one tittle of the law to fail.[91]

The son of Satan, on the other hand, intends to change times and law.[92] He has attempted to manipulate the Ten

86 Luke 5:20-25
87 Luke 13:11-16
88 Revelation 13:5, 6

89 Hebrews 8:1, 2; 4:15
90 Matthew 5:17, 18
91 Luke 16:17
92 Daniel 7:25

Commandments so that man might worship his father, Satan. He sought to do away with the second commandment, which forbids idol worship,[93] and to change the fourth commandment regarding the keeping holy of the Sabbath of the Lord God Almighty, the Creator of the Universe.[94]

Our merciful Savior, the Son of God, Immanuel, came to give His life to ransom us from sin and the grave.[95] After He had by Himself purged our sins, the Son of God sat down at the right hand of the Majesty on high.[96] There is one God and one Mediator between God and men, the Man Christ Jesus.[97] Therefore He is also able to save to the uttermost those who come to God through Him, since He always lives to make intercession for them.[98]

In contrast, the son of Satan has consistently persecuted the saints of the Most High, made war against them and overcame

them.[99] Authority was given him over every tribe, tongue, and nation. He established a counterfeit priesthood, through which he causes all who dwell on the earth to worship him, whose names have not been written in the Book of Life of the Lamb slain from the foundation of the world.[100]

Beloved, rejoice that your names are written in the Book of Life.[101] We know that we are of God, and the whole world lies under the sway of the wicked one.[102] For this reason I will not be negligent to remind you always of these things, though you know and are established in the present truth.[103]

We are of God. He who knows God hears us; he who is not of God does not hear us. By this we know the spirit of truth and the spirit of error.[104] Because we are of the truth, we need not fear, for perfect love casts out all fear.[105] Elect of God, we know that the Son of God has come and has

93 Exodus 20:4-6;
   Deuteronomy 5:8-10
94 Exodus 20:8-11;
   Deuteronomy 5:12-15
95 I Timothy 2:6
96 Hebrews 1:3
97 I Timothy 2:5
98 Hebrews 7:25

99 Daniel 7:25; Revelation 13:7
100 Revelation 13:7, 8
101 Luke 10:20
102 I John 5:19
103 II Peter 1:12
104 I John 4:6
105 I John 4:18

given us an understanding, that we may know Him who is true; and we are in Him who is true, in His Son Jesus Christ. This is the true God and eternal life.[106]

We also know that God has promised us wisdom,[107] that we may know Him who is true, and we may identify him who is false, and that we might not be deluded by the father of lies nor by the son of Satan. That you be not deceived I declare unto you who this son of Satan is according to the Word of God.

As I share this with you, precious children of God, you should understand that the Word of God does not refer to specific individuals; it speaks of spiritual realities. For we do not wrestle against flesh and blood, but against principalities, against powers, against the rulers of the darkness of this age, against spiritual hosts of wickedness in the heavenly places.[108]

This horrible beast resembles his father, the dragon, who is Satan. He represents a powerful earthly kingdom that is an amalgamation of all the other worldly empires that preceded it and opposed the kingdom of God. When convenient, the son of Satan will mingle truth with lies in order to advance his temporal reign. His throne, power, and authority were given to him by his father, the devil.

At one point in the history of this religious kingdom, it received what appeared to be a death blow, yet it was then miraculously healed. Following this astounding false resurrection, all the world marvels and most of the people on earth worship this son of Satan. In so doing, those that worship the beast worship the dragon; many are unwittingly worshiping Satan.

This religio-political power was granted an opportunity to demonstrate to all of heaven what the universe would be like if ruled by Satan. Through his vice-regent and son, Satan was given authority to rule for one thousand two hundred and sixty years. Throughout this time, and even now, the son of Satan claims to be God on earth. During much of this

---

106 I John 5:20
107 James 1:5
108 Ephesians 6:12

long period of darkness, this beast carried on a war against the people of God, persecuting, torturing, and slaughtering our brethren without mercy.

The son of Satan tries to usurp the place of the Son of God by creating a false priesthood on earth. Through this fallacious priesthood, he blasphemes God by claiming the authority to forgive sins. He blasphemes the character of God in heaven through his deceptive practices and false doctrines. Satan uses his son to attempt a change to the Ten Commandments, which were written on stone with the finger of God,[109] and are to be written on our hearts by His Spirit.[110] Through his son, the devil tries to modify the Commandments in an effort to cause people to worship him through idols and the sun.

O my dear beloved fellow believer, surely by now you realize that this Satanic masterpiece of deception is truly anti-Christ. The son of Satan is the Papacy of the Roman Catholic Church.

That the son of Satan is indeed the Papacy is confirmed by her sordid history. The Papacy ascended to power shortly after the collapse of the Roman Empire. When Emperor Constantine wanted to gain political advantage, he and his army were "baptized" into this apostate faith. It was this same Constantine that demanded that all be required to stop their labors on the venerable day of the sun, rather than rest on the Sabbath of the Lord God. Later the Emperor Justinian signed a decree ordaining that the Bishop of Rome was the head of all the churches. In 538 A.D., when three other contending powers were removed from Roman territory – the three horns that Daniel saw in vision[111] - the Roman Catholic Church began her tyrannical reign of terror upon the earth. For 1,260 years this oppressor ruled Europe, raging a violent war against the people of God. Untold millions suffered at the hands of this demonic power who claims to be the vicar of Christ. Even now this blasphemous power asserts that it is God on earth.

---

109 Exodus 31:18; Deuteronomy 9:10
110 Jeremiah 31:31-33; Hebrews 8:10

111 Daniel 7:24

Any visit to a Catholic church reveals the confessional booth, in which the priest contends that the sinner should confess his sins to man. This same priest then claims to have the authority to exonerate the individual from all vices, usually in exchange for an act of penance or finances. That same man, in the course of the preparation of the mass, asserts that he has the power to create God when praying over a wafer! After lifting it up in offering, while facing the idol, he then breaks the wafer and claims to have crucified the Son of God afresh. The Bible says that Jesus died once for all,[112] yet this idolatrous system claims to not only create God, but to kill Him repeatedly every day. This is what is actually perpetrated by the son of Satan in the name of God! Outrageous blasphemy!

It was through his vice-regent on earth that Satan attempted to change the commandments of God. The second commandment prohibits idol worship in any form and promises merciful blessings to those who keep the commandments of God. The Roman Catholic Church has sought to remove this commandment from the heart of man and replaced it with the worship of images made by human hands. It is not listed as one of the commandments in either its churches or in its catechisms.

Dear beloved fellow believers who until now have been in the Catholic church, I have spoken openly to you, my heart is wide open. You are not restricted by me, but you are restricted by your own affections. What fellowship has righteousness with lawlessness? And what communion has light with darkness? And what accord has Christ with Satan? And what agreement has the temple of God with idols?

You are the temple of the living God. As God has said, I will dwell in them and walk among them. I will be their God, and they shall be My people. Therefore, Come out from among them and be separate, says the Lord. Do not touch what is unclean, and I will receive you. I will be a Father to you, and you shall be My sons and daughters, says the Lord Almighty.[113]

---

112 *Hebrews 10:10*

113 *II Corinthians 6:11, 14-18*

Further, remember that the fourth commandment is intended to be a blessing to those who labor throughout the week. God ordains that we keep the seventh day of the week as a holy Sabbath, because it is this day that He blessed and sanctified when He rested from creation. Satan has used the Roman Catholic Church to try to manipulate this commandment, and require man to worship on the first day of the week, Sunday. In so doing, man is called to worship the created, the sun, instead of the Creator, the Lord God Almighty.

Brothers and sisters in Christ, the information I share with you is not a well kept secret. It is public information. In fact, as you enter most Catholic churches you will often be greeted by an idol, usually above the doorway. Likewise, frequently there is some emblem on the building giving homage to the created object of worship within: the sun. Please verify the truth of what I share with the reality of these houses of worship.

Throughout the Dark Ages, those who opposed the work of the son of Satan faced the rack, the sword, the dungeon and the stake. As the light of the Word of God became available to people when the Reformation began to dawn, the fires of persecution were enflamed to an even greater fury. The superstitious bondage that the Papacy held over the hearts and souls of men was being broken by the power of the Holy Bible. Finally in 1798, the armies of Napoleon under the direction of General Berthier, marched into the Vatican, deposed the Pope, and took him captive to France. As God foresaw, the son of Satan was allowed to rule for his predetermined period of 3 ½ prophetic times, or 42 prophetic months, or 1260 prophetic days (538-1798) and no more. The deadly wound was inflicted exactly when God predicted it would be: at the end of 1,260 years of deception and disgrace.

Consider the situation of the world today. It was prophesied that after the deadly wound inflicted upon this beast was healed, all the world would

THE TWO TRINITIES: FATHER, SON, SPIRIT

GOD THE FATHER
– THE MOST HIGH –

Merciful, gracious, abounding in goodness and truth

The Father of light

GOD THE SON
– JESUS CHRIST –

Receives authority from His Father, Almighty God

He is crucified, yet resurrected

When we worship Jesus, we worship the Father

Ministers on earth for $3^1/_2$ literal years

Jesus was God on earth

As God, Jesus forgives sin

Jesus kept the commandments

Jesus gave His life that we might have eternal life

GOD THE SPIRIT
– HOLY SPIRIT –

Given by God the Father

Comes down like fire at Pentecost

Leads us into all truth

Inspired the authors of the Bible

Leads to the seal of God

SATAN THE DRAGON

Wants to be the Most High

The father of lies

THE SON OF SATAN
– ANTICHRIST –

Receives authority from his father, the devil

Receives deadly wound that is healed

Those who worship this beast are actually worshiping Satan

Has authority for $3^1/_2$ prophetic years

Claims to be God on earth

Blasphemes by claiming to forgive sin

Seeks to destroy the commandments

Son of Satan comes to destroy those who worship God

SPIRIT OF SATAN
– UNHOLY SPIRIT –

Authority from dragon, Satan

Has an unholy Pentecost

Leads into confusion and lies

People trust their feelings, not the Bible

Leads to the mark of the beast

marvel and follow the son of Satan; all except those whose names are written in the Book of Life of the Lamb slain from the foundation of the world.[114] The power of the Papacy has been on the ascendancy for many years, and it has stealthily been working its way back to a position of global dominance. It is now, in our time, without doubt the most powerful spiritual voice on earth. Again we see clearly that the Word of God is true.

After describing the work of Satan and his son, our brother John goes on to describe another beast that comes up out of the earth, and he had two horns like a lamb and spoke like a dragon. And he exercises all the authority of the first beast in his presence, and causes the earth and those who dwell in it to worship the first beast, whose deadly wound was healed.[115]

This beast has two horns like a lamb, but speaks like a dragon. Who is the dragon? That old serpent, the devil, and Satan.[116] This beast has gentle horns like a lamb, yet speaks like a serpent with forked tongue.

Remember beloved, the Holy Spirit that you received comes from the Father and is given by Jesus; it is the Spirit of truth.[117] Conversely, the Bible reveals that soon the son of Satan will have an idol erected in his honor by a beast that is filled with the unholy spirit. This beast represents a system established through an unholy spirit who exercises the same coercive authority as the son of Satan. Just as Jesus received His authority from His Father, so too does the son of Satan receive his power from his father, the devil. Jesus promised to give us the Holy Spirit to guide us into all truth as revealed in Scripture.[118] In contrast, this unholy spirit comes into the hearts and minds of people to turn them away from the Bible and to lead them into lies and confusion.

When the true Holy Spirit comes into our lives, He teaches us those things that Jesus said and taught in the Bible, and leads us to worship Jesus.[119]

---

114 Revelation 13:8
115 Revelation 13:11, 12
116 Revelation 12:9

117 John 15:26
118 John 16:13
119 John 14:26; 16:14

When we worship Jesus, we are worshipping God the Father.[120]

As a counterfeit to the true, Satan sends the unholy spirit that leads people away from the Bible, and for this reason it is also referred to in the Scriptures as a false prophet.[121] This lying spirit causes people to worship the son of Satan.[122] And as we saw before, those who worship the son of Satan are actually worshipping Satan.[123]

The Bible further describes this beast as being able to perform great signs, so that he even makes fire come down from heaven on the earth in the sight of men.[124] Beloved, you may recall that fire came down from heaven on several occasions in the Scriptures.

The first time fire fell from heaven was when by faith Abel sacrificed a lamb and his offering was accepted by God.[125] Another time was when Solomon dedicated the temple in Jerusalem and the presence of God filled the sanctuary.[126] Of course we remember the powerful experience on Mount Carmel when our brother Elijah challenged the prophets of Baal, the Babylonian sun god. Through the faithfulness of Elijah, the God of heaven showed that He alone is God, and that He should not be confused with the idolatrous worship of the sun.[127] All of these experiences share something in common: the fire fell from heaven when the sacrifice was accepted. Abel's sacrifice was accepted; Solomon's sacrifice was accepted; Elijah's sacrifice was accepted.

The last time that the Bible records that fire fell from heaven was when the disciples were gathered together in an upper room after Jesus ascended back to heaven. They prayed, confessed their sins, and prepared to receive the promised Comforter.[128] The Bible tells us that the Holy

120 II John 1:9
121 Revelation 19:20
122 Revelation 13:12
123 Revelation 13:4
124 Revelation 13:13
125 Genesis 4:4
126 II Chronicles 7:1
127 I Kings 18:36-39
128 John 15:26; Acts 1:4

THE DRAGON, THE BEAST, AND THE FALSE PROPHET

Spirit fell like fire from heaven on Pentecost. [129]

The feast of Pentecost was fifty days following the Sabbath of Passover.[130] In this case it was fifty days since the Sabbath that Jesus rested in the tomb before His resurrection on the first of the week.[131] For forty days following His resurrection He demonstrated to His disciples that He had indeed risen from the dead.[132] Then Jesus went to heaven, and as the first fruits of God, His sacrifice was accepted by the Father. In response, the Father poured the Holy Spirit upon His waiting, praying people. Jesus promised that His Father would send the Comforter,[133] and instructed His disciples to wait in Jerusalem until they received Him.[134] In fulfillment of this promise, God gave the Spirit of truth in a glorious display of fire power. On Pentecost, fifty days following Passover, God demonstrated that the sacrifice of the Lamb of God was accepted, and in response He sent fire from heaven.

In the Scriptures God reveals a parallel between the literal time of the ministry of the Son of God and the prophetic period allotted to the son of Satan. In like manner, as with the outpouring of the true Holy Spirit, so the counterfeit unholy spirit comes in its time. We saw that the son of Satan, the Papacy, received its deadly wound at the end of its prophetic time to reign (1,260 years) in 1798. When the Pope was taken captive, he received his deadly wound; it was the time of his so-called sacrifice.

In the same way, the unholy spirit would begin to be poured out fifty prophetic days [years] after the sacrifice of the son of Satan. Remember the Biblical principle of interpretation that in prophecy a day is equal to a year.[135] When we add fifty years to 1798, the time that the deadly wound was inflicted upon the papacy, it brings us

---

129 Acts 2:1-4
130 Leviticus 23:15, 16
131 Luke 23:53-24:6
132 Acts 1:3
133 John 14:16, 16:7
134 Acts 1:4, 8

135 Numbers 14:34; Ezekiel 4:6

to the time of the beginning of the false Pentecost in 1848. The unholy fire fell when the Satanic sacrifice was accepted.

O my dear brethren, chosen from before the foundation of the world, it was at this time a movement began that is spreading across the globe like fire. Back in 1848, two sisters of the Fox family began communicating with unseen spirits in upstate New York. At the time this movement began, it was called spiritualism. Today the more common manifestation is when people invite these spirits to take control of them in an effort to achieve a supernaturally ecstatic experience.

When the fire of God fell from heaven upon the awaiting disciples, they were given an extraordinary gift to help them communicate the gospel of Jesus Christ: each of them began to preach in different languages that they had never known before.[136] Beloved, please read this entire account in your Bibles. It is found in the second chapter of the book of Acts.

The disciples were filled with the Holy Spirit. They were given the ability to share the message of the incarnate, crucified, resurrected and ascended Christ with the multitudes assembled in Jerusalem for the Feast of Weeks, or Pentecost.[137] The people gathered there were from many different countries, speaking different languages, yet they each heard and understood the good news of salvation in their own mother tongues because the disciples preached in their own native languages.[138] The disciples were speaking in genuine languages these foreigners to Jerusalem could understand so that others would learn to trust in Jesus of Nazareth as the Messiah. The Holy Spirit fell like fire upon those who had been with Jesus and were waiting for the Helper. The Holy Spirit was sent so that they could accomplish the task that Jesus had given them when He ascended into heaven: to share the gospel with all nations, kindred, tongue and people.[139]

---

136 Acts 2:4

137 Acts 2:6; Exodus 34:22
138 Acts 2:6-11
139 Acts 1:8; Matthew 28:18-20; Rev. 14:7

Elect of God, the arch-deceiver has a counterfeit to the true Holy Spirit, and many well-meaning brethren are being led astray by his sophistries. I share this in love that you be not deceived and destroyed. The unholy spirit is a very subtle deception that seeks to manipulate our emotions and our spiritual sensitivity.

When the unholy spirit comes, instead of causing the people of God to share the gospel in different languages for the glory of God, he produces an unintelligible language that no one can understand. Satan uses this unholy spirit to cause people to trust their feelings rather than the Word of God, and leads people away from the God of heaven.

O my beloved brethren, especially those who have been ensnared by this subtle delusion, I plead with you: search the Word as did the Bereans. Ask God to confirm to you that what is shared here is consistent with light of the Bible. When they say to you,

Seek those who are mediums and wizards, who whisper and mutter [in incomprehensible noises], should not a people seek their God? Should they seek the dead on behalf of the living? To the law and to the testimony! If they do not speak according to this word, it is because there is no light in them.[140]

In these last days people are seeking to be filled with a spirit, but they know not from where this spirit comes. Be wise, dear beloved. Test the spirits. God is a God of decency and order, [141] and He is not glorified when people claim to be filled with His presence and boast of being able to speak in nonsensical gibberish.

The encouraging thing to remember is that from the beginning God knew that in the end time a terrible apostasy would take place among the professed people of God.[142] God has warned us that this would happen. He foretold that the coming of the lawless one is according to the working of Satan, with all power, signs,

---

140 Isaiah 8:19, 20
141 I Corinthians 14:40
142 II Timothy 3:1-5

and lying wonders, and with all unrighteous deception among those who perish, because they did not receive the love of the truth, that they might be saved. And for this reason God will send them strong delusion, that they should believe the lie, that they all may be condemned who did not believe the truth but had pleasure in unrighteousness.[143]

Beloved, I earnestly plead with you: examine yourselves as to whether you are in the faith. Test yourselves. Do you not know yourselves, that Jesus Christ is in you?—unless indeed you are disqualified.[144] Do you not only believe the truth, but do you love it? Do you cherish the Word of God above all others? – above television, money, the Internet, newspapers, magazines, sports, fashion, and all other worldly interests. Is the truth of God more precious to you than your own feelings?

O my brethren united through the shed blood of the Son of God, buy the truth, and do not sell it, also wisdom and instruction and understanding.[145] You need

not accept the opinion of man for truth. Love the truth; read the Bible; trust what is written in the Scriptures. Many of our friends are accepting the strong delusion because they do not really love the truth. Beloved, we can do nothing against the truth, but for the truth.[146]

The Holy Spirit is the spirit of truth who convicts us of sin, righteousness and judgment through the Word of God.[147] The Holy Spirit points us away from ourselves and invites us to look to Jesus as our Savior.[148]

The unholy spirit does not condemn sin, does not bring judgment, and causes unrighteous confusion. This unholy spirit creates a situation in the mind of man that persuades everyone to do what is right in his own eyes.[149] Some of these people claim that because they have this spirit, they are a law unto themselves and therefore put aside the law of God. Jesus tells those who claim to be His disciples yet practice lawlessness that He will have to

---

143 II Thessalonians 2:9-12
144 II Corinthians 13:5
145 Proverbs 23:23

146 II Corinthians 13:8
147 John 16:8-11
148 John 16:14, 15
149 Judges 21:25

refuse them entrance into the kingdom of God. O beloved, may He not have to say this of me and you.[150]

Rather than looking to Jesus, men turn inward in their devotions when possessed of this spirit in an effort to edify themselves. The character present in the father of lies is often demonstrated in those who possess this unholy spirit. It is a character centered in I, I, I.[151] Rather than being God and Christ centered, based upon the Holy Scriptures, this spirit is self-centered based upon feelings. In this way people are deceived much as was Eve in the garden of Eden: she sought to have an experience that she did not then possess (to be made wise), and she trusted her feelings rather than relying upon what God had said. She fell for the lie that Satan is perpetuating among the people of God even today: you will not die if you disobey; in fact, you will be like God.[152]

Often times in prayer people controlled by this spirit will directly contradict the counsel of Jesus and use vain repetitions as the heathen do, for they think that they will be heard for their many words.[153] It may be that they repeat, Hallelujah, Praise the Lord, or Jesus, over and over; it is still vain repetition.

This unholy spirit is indeed a crafty delusion, invented by the devil to deceive those who dwell on the earth by those signs which he was granted to do in the sight of the beast.[154] Not only do people speak in confusing unintelligible tongues, but Satan deceives people through miracles and signs. He performs these signs through his unholy spirit operating in those who are taken captive to do his will.

I ask you, chosen of heaven: will the God who forbids idolatry in any form cause statues of Mary to weep blood? Will the God of the Bible, the Creator of heaven and earth, allow His glory to be given to an image of wood, metal or stone? No, He will not.

Dear fellow believers, you know

---

150 *Matthew 7:21-23*
151 *Isaiah 14:12-14*
152 *Genesis 3:1-6*

153 *Matthew 6:7*
154 *Revelation 13:14*

that the demons have power to perform miracles, just as they did in counterfeiting the miracles that God performed in Egypt.[155] Does Satan have the power to heal people? He has the power to make people sick, and then take away that sickness when it suits his purpose. He uses this power to advance his purposes in waging war against the kingdom of God.

Many modern faith healers stimulate interest in their programs by advertising great powers of healing, but often they are nothing more than charlatans seeking to take money from gullible people. Nevertheless, some of these covetous manipulators are ignorantly used by the authority of Satan to perform some great enchantment. The God of health and healing does not cause miracles to happen for people who willfully persist in the sins that caused their sickness. No; when Jesus healed people, He also told them not to continue in sin.[156]

Elect of God, Jesus Himself has warned us: take heed that no one deceives you. For many will come in My name, saying, 'I am He,' and will deceive many. For false christs and false prophets will rise and show signs and wonders to deceive, if possible, even the elect. But take heed; see, I have told you all things beforehand.[157]

We find an incident in the Bible that helps us to understand this satanic spirit. Shortly after the flood all men spoke one language. Although Noah was still living and could testify to the mercy of the one true God, sinful men did not trust in the grace of God nor in the manner of salvation that He provides. Instead men sought to edify themselves by building a monument to make a name for themselves. They started to set up a tower, an idol, for their own glory. The languages of these people were confused because they sought to worship themselves. God prevented them from accomplishing their work of idolatry. This place is called Babel, or Babylon, which means, confusion.[158]

Now again in the last moments

---

155 Exodus 7:11, 22; 8:7
156 John 5:14; 8:11
157 Mark 13:5, 6, 22, 23
158 Genesis 11:1-9

of earth's history, we see that the past is repeated, and again, God knows the end from the beginning.

The Bible reveals that soon the son of Satan will have an image erected in his honor by the beast that is filled with the unholy spirit. All those who bow down to this image will be worshiping not only the son of Satan but will be honoring the father of lies, Satan himself. We must understand this invention of the devil and his plan to cause all to receive his mark through this hellish beast.

Before we examine the mark of the beast, and contrast it with the seal of God, we need to listen to the message given by God to prepare His children for His kingdom in these last days. This message is the last warning message that the world will hear. Beloved, how you respond to this message determines whether you receive the seal of God, or the mark of the beast. How you respond to this message determines your eternal destiny.

Take heed to yourselves, lest your heart be deceived, and you turn aside and serve other gods and worship them.[159] Therefore take careful heed to yourselves, that you love the Lord your God.[160]

Take heed...

---

159 *Deuteronomy 11:16*
160 *Joshua 23:11*

FEAR GOD AND GIVE GLORY TO HIM

John, called to be a servant of Jesus Christ through the will of God, to the church of God which is living in the time of the end, to those who are sanctified in Christ Jesus, called to be saints, with all who in every place call on the name of Jesus Christ our Lord: Grace to you and peace from God our Father and the Lord Jesus Christ.[1]

Beloved, God has in these last days revealed mysteries hidden since the time of Daniel,[2] but opened now to us who live in the last days. From before the foundation of the world God knew the end from the beginning. He knew that Lucifer would choose to become Satan because of his pride. God foresaw that, in making His creatures to be free to choose whether they would worship Him or not, God would have to someday sacrifice Himself for the sins of the world. He also knew that Satan would counterfeit the kingdom of God on earth to try to entice human beings to worship the created rather than the Creator.[3]

In the Bible it is written that in the last moments of time there is a tremendous spiritual battle for the control of the hearts and minds of people. The Holy Spirit is seeking to draw men into the kingdom of God and to seal them for eternity.[4] At the same time, Satan uses his unholy spirit to lead people to reject God, His Word, and His law, and to receive a mark indicating their allegiance to him.[5] Which authority we give our loyalty to demonstrates who we worship and determines whether we receive everlasting life or suffer the consequences of eternal damnation.

Before every mind is sealed, before the final decision is made by each searching heart, God sends a special message

---

1 *I Corinthians 1:2,3*
2 *Daniel 12:9*

3 *Romans 1:25*
4 *Eph. 1:13; 4:30; Rev. 14:1-5*
5 *Revelation 13:16-18*

to prepare the people for His kingdom. That warning is given by three messengers acting in unity, and is ultimately joined by a final heavenly voice. Together they declare that the end of all things is rapidly fulfilling, and the inauguration of the kingdom of God is at hand.

The first of the angelic messengers appears flying in the midst of heaven, having the everlasting gospel to preach to those who dwell on the earth—to every nation, tribe, tongue, and people—saying with a loud voice, Fear God and give glory to Him, for the hour of His judgment has come; and worship Him who made heaven and earth, the sea and springs of water.

And another angel follows, saying, Babylon is fallen, is fallen, that great city, because she has made all nations drink of the wine of the wrath of her fornication.

Then a third angel follows them, saying with a loud voice, If anyone worships the beast and his image, and receives his mark

on his forehead or on his hand, he himself shall also drink of the wine of the wrath of God, which is poured out full strength into the cup of His indignation. He shall be tormented with fire and brimstone in the presence of the holy angels and in the presence of the Lamb. And the smoke of their torment ascends forever and ever; and they have no rest day or night, who worship the beast and his image, and whoever receives the mark of his name. Here is the patience of the saints; here are those who keep the commandments of God and the faith of Jesus.[6]

The final warning is given to the inhabitants of the earth as these three messengers complete their ministry in boldly proclaiming the heavenly decrees. Another angel comes down from heaven, having great authority, and the earth was illuminated with his glory. And he cries mightily with a loud voice, saying, Babylon the great is fallen, is fallen, and has become a dwelling place of demons, a prison for every foul spirit, and a cage for every unclean and hated bird! For all the nations have drunk of

_____

6 *Revelation 14:6-12*

the wine of the wrath of her fornication, the kings of the earth have committed fornication with her, and the merchants of the earth have become rich through the abundance of her luxury.

And I heard another voice from heaven saying, Come out of her, my people, lest you share in her sins, and lest you receive of her plagues. For her sins have reached to heaven, and God has remembered her iniquities.[7]

Beloved, it is essential that we understand these messages. How we read, hear and respond to these messages determines whether we are sealed by God as His, or we are marked by Satan as his. If we receive the seal of God we will inherit eternal life; if we choose the mark of the beast we will go to hell. Watch therefore, and pray always that you may be counted worthy to escape all these things that will come to pass, and to stand before the Son of Man.[8] And what I say to you, I say to all: Watch![9]

The first angel's message is: Fear God and give glory to Him, for the hour of His judgment has come; and worship Him who made heaven and earth, the sea and springs of water.[10] We must understand who it is we worship, why we worship, and how we are to worship.

We are called to honor, reverence and worship God and to give Him glory. Who is the God that calls us to worship Him? It is the Creator, our Maker and King. We worship Him because He is our Creator, and it is He who gives us life. He is not only our Creator, but also the Creator of heaven and earth, the sea and springs of water. This call to worship identifies the God of the Bible as the Creator, and refers to how we are to honor Him who is the one true God.

Our heavenly Father gives explicit instructions concerning His worship. They are found in the Bible where He is recognized as the Lord who made the heavens and the earth, the sea, and all that is in them. God wrote the Ten Commandments with His own finger, and in the fourth commandment he

---

7 *Revelation 18:1-5*
8 *Luke 21:36*
9 *Mark 13:37*

10 *Revelation 14:7*

reminds us that when He had finished Creation, He rested the seventh day. Therefore the Lord blessed the Sabbath day and hallowed it.[11]

Many of our fellow Christian believers simply follow tradition without understanding the importance of what they are doing when called to worship the God of heaven. Jesus declares concerning such: This people honors Me with their lips, but their heart is far from Me. And in vain they worship Me, teaching as doctrines the commandments of men. For laying aside the commandment of God, you hold the tradition of men.[12] Many people ignorantly transgress the commandment of God because they have not understood these truths. Others have given heed to the words of men instead of discovering what the Bible says concerning these matters. Earlier we read that the first angel's message is a call to worship God in the manner which He commands, which beckons us to keep holy the seventh-day Sabbath. Brothers and sisters, we ought to obey God rather than men.[13] Jesus tells us that if we love Him, we will keep His commandments.[14]

Those who do not worship God in the manner that He commands can be understood to be idolaters. An idolater is someone who worships something that they make themselves rather than worshiping the Creator who made them. This object of worship can be a literal idol, a preoccupation with human theories, or a clinging to an idea that is contrary to what God has declared in His Word. Essentially people who adhere to these objects are worshipping themselves because they have made their own opinion into a god, and they do not worship the God of the Bible.

The first angel's message also declares that the hour of judgment is come. Dear friends, many people are confused about the judgment of God. Yet I want you to consider one thought that should be perfectly clear. When the Son of God comes with all the angels of heaven to take the redeemed with

---

11 *Exodus 20:11*
12 *Mark 7:6-8*

13 *Acts 5:29*
14 *John 14:15*

them to the eternal kingdom,[15] they do not decide when they arrive to this planet who will go with them. Rather, as the Scriptures reveal, the judgment has taken place beforehand in heaven.[16] Judgment has been determined in heaven before the angels come with Jesus to reap His harvest.

For this reason there comes a time, just before the second advent, when Jesus declares: He who is unjust, let him be unjust still; he who is filthy, let him be filthy still; he who is righteous, let him be righteous still; he who is holy, let him be holy still. And behold, I am coming quickly, and My reward is with Me, to give to every one according to his work. I am the Alpha and the Omega, the Beginning and the End, the First and the Last. Blessed are those who do His commandments, that they may have the right to the tree of life, and may enter through the gates into the city.[17]

The second angel's message is:

Babylon is fallen, is fallen, that great city, because she has made all nations drink of the wine of the wrath of her fornication.[18] We saw earlier that the city of Babylon was constructed by people whose hearts were set on rebellion against God. They did not trust what God said, but put their confidence in their own opinions and what they could do to save themselves. The result was that God caused them to become deluded in their languages, and their effort at self-exaltation ceased.

Throughout the Bible the history of Babel [Babylon] is one of apostasy and rebellion. Babylon was first built by Nimrod,[19] the father of a line of renegades and God-rejecting children. It was at Babel that the tongues of men became confused because of their heaven insulting idolatry. And in these last days, spiritual Babylon will erect an idolatrous image to the son of Satan, commanding that whoever transgresses its decree will be threatened with death.[20]

15 Matthew 24:30, 31
16 Daniel 7:9,10,13,14
17 Revelation 22:11-14

18 Revelation 14:8
19 Genesis 10:10
20 Revelation 13:15

Babylon has always been a place where those who worshipped the inventions of their own minds oppose and persecute those who worship the God of heaven. Babylon has always been the center of confusion and coercion, where the religious authorities fornicate with the government powers in an effort to eliminate those that do not bow to their bestial decrees.

So it will be in these last days. The angelic messenger goes forth with the authority of heaven and declares that Babylon – this confused religious system mingled with the power of the government – is fallen. God has judged this system of deceptive scheming, because it has fallen into the abyss of sin.

The message given by the third angel is the strongest warning given by God in the entire Bible. He goes forward with urgency and intensity declaring that, If anyone worships the beast and his image, and receives his mark on his forehead or on his hand, he himself shall also drink of the wine of the wrath of God, which is poured out full strength into the cup of His indignation. He shall be tormented with fire and brimstone in the presence of the holy angels and in the presence of the Lamb. And the smoke of their torment ascends forever and ever; and they have no rest day or night, who worship the beast and his image, and whoever receives the mark of his name. Here is the patience of the saints; here are those who keep the commandments of God and the faith of Jesus.[21]

Beloved, we shall clearly identify the mark of the beast and the seal of God. Those who receive the mark of the beast will be consumed in the fires of hell and the second death. Those who receive the seal of God follow the Lamb withersoever He goes throughout eternity.[22] O that we might be sealed by the Spirit of God and saved in His eternal kingdom.[23] I beseech you, beloved, that you give heed to these few words that I write unto you.[24]

21 *Revelation 14:9-12*
22 *Revelation 14:4*
23 *Ephesians 4:30; Revelation 7:3; 14:1*
24 *Hebrews 13:22*

The End from the Beginning

By your patience possess
your souls.[25]

---

25 Luke 21:19

Chapter Eight
OUR GOD WHOM WE SERVE IS ABLE

John, to the church in the world yet not of the world,[1] in God our Father and the Lord Jesus Christ: Grace to you and peace from God our Father and the Lord Jesus Christ.

I am bound to thank God always for you, brethren, as it is fitting, because your faith grows exceedingly, and the love of every one of you all abounds toward each other, so that I shall boast of you among the churches of God for your patience and faith in all your persecutions and tribulations that you will have to endure, which is manifest evidence of the righteous judgment of God, that you may be counted worthy of the kingdom of God, for which you also suffer; since it is a righteous thing with God to repay with tribulation those who shall trouble you, and to give you who are troubled rest with me when the Lord

Jesus is revealed from heaven with His mighty angels, in flaming fire taking vengeance on those who do not know God, and on those who do not obey the gospel of our Lord Jesus Christ.[2]

Brethren, we have seen how the enemy of God and man has sought to counterfeit the ministry of the family of God. Satan seeks to usurp the Father, he establishes a false son and breathes out an unholy spirit. God gave us His Word that we might be prepared for His kingdom, and so that we would not be deceived by any pretenders for our loyalty. In these last hours, the devil knows that he has a short time[3] and so he does his best to confuse and destroy the people of God. Yet we need not be afraid, for He who is the Alpha and the Omega,[4] the Beginning and the End,[5] has promised that He will

---

1 *John 17:14-16*

2 *II Thessalonians 1:1-8*
3 *Revelation 12:12*
4 *Revelation 1:8, 11*
5 *Revelation 21:6; 22:13*

be with us even to the end of the world.[6]

The Word of God tells us that in the final moments of time before the return of our Lord Jesus Christ there will be only two groups of people on the earth: those who worship God and receive His seal; and those who worship Satan and receive his mark. Beloved, I would not have you be ignorant of this mystery that has been revealed in these last days that each of you might choose to worship God in Spirit and in truth.[7]

Earlier we learned that an amalgamated beast rose up out of the sea, having seven heads and ten hours. Through the Scriptures we understand clearly that this beast is a representation of the son of Satan, who is the Papacy. Further, we then saw that another beast, with lamb-like horns, arose from the earth. The Bible reveals that the religious aspect of this beast is likened to an unholy spirit, which represents those systems of worship that have fallen into

confusion because they rely upon tradition and emotional passions instead of the Word of God. We will discuss the political aspect of this second beast after some time.

The Bible says that this unholy spirit will tell those who dwell on the earth to make an image to the beast who was wounded by the sword and lived, that is, to the son of Satan.

He was granted power to give breath [spirit] to the image of the beast, that the image of the beast should both speak and cause as many as would not worship the image of the beast to be killed. He causes all, both small and great, rich and poor, free and slave, to receive a mark on their right hand or on their foreheads, and that no one may buy or sell except one who has the mark or the name of the beast, or the number of his name.

Here is wisdom. Let him who has understanding calculate the

---

6 Matthew 28:20
7 John 4:23

number of the beast, for it is the number of a man: His number is six hundred and sixty and six.[8]

O my beloved brethren in Christ Jesus, the Word of God counsels us that this mystery requires wisdom and understanding, and therefore I urge you to pray even right now that the Holy Spirit may abide in your hearts by faith, and that you may be filled with the knowledge of His will in all wisdom and spiritual understanding.[9]

Our Lord has not left us alone,[10] nor has He left us without sufficient information in His Word to understand this mystery. If anyone wants to do His will, he shall know concerning the doctrine, whether it is from God or whether I speak on My own authority.[11] He who is of God hears God's words; but those who are not of God do not hear.[12]

There is much speculation in the world concerning this beast, his mark, and the number six

hundred, sixty and six. Some of it is reasonable; much of it is nonsensical. The thing that almost all of these speculations have in common is that they are not Biblical. O beloved, in a matter of such importance concerning our eternal destiny, certainly we can trust God to decipher this mystery in His Holy Word.

The God of heaven bids us to calculate the number of the beast, for it is the number of a man: his number is six hundred and sixty and six.[13] God gives us a key to unlocking this mystery, and it is found in this mystifying number.

To comprehend what God wants us to know about this beast and his mark, we should look in the Bible for the places where this number, six hundred sixty and six, occur. There are only three other verses in Scripture that contain this number other than the one already quoted from Revelation. Two of these verses say exactly the same thing but in different books of the Bible. The

---

8 Revelation 13:14-18
9 Colossians 1:9
10 John 14:18
11 John 7:17
12 John 8:47

13 Revelation 13:18

verses read: The weight of gold that came to Solomon yearly was six hundred and sixty and six talents of gold.[14]

Another verse, with an introduction so we understand what the verse refers to, is: Now these are the people of the province who came back from the captivity, of those who had been carried away, whom Nebuchadnezzar the king of Babylon had carried away to Babylon, and who returned to Jerusalem and Judah, everyone to his own city... the people of Adonikam, six hundred and sixty and six.[15]

We have already noted that the unholy spirit sets up an image to the son of Satan, and commands everyone to worship it and take the mark of the son of Satan, and that a key aspect to understand this mystery is the number six hundred and sixty and six.[16]

When these seemingly disjointed verses are looked at in the proper way, it becomes clear that God is answering our prayer for wisdom and

understanding in this matter. From the one verse in Revelation and its context, we see that we need to look in the Bible for a story in which an idol is set up, and those who stay loyal to God are threatened with death. From the information that is mentioned twice in Scripture, a large amount of gold is involved in this mystery. We learn from the last text that the King of Babylon has taken God's people captive, but that ultimately God delivers them.

Beloved, there is a story in the Bible in which King Nebuchadnezzar of Babylon takes God's people captive, demands that they worship an idol, made from a significant amount of gold, most likely taken from the temple constructed by Solomon, and declares that whoever does not worship this idol will be thrown into the furnace to die. Thankfully our Savior Jesus goes into the fires with His faithful ones and delivers them.[17] Hallelujah!

Dear brethren, God is leading us to understand the mystery of the mark of the beast through

14 I Kings 10:14; II Chronicles 9:13
15 Ezra 2:1, 13
16 Revelation 13:15-18

17 Daniel 3

this story that is in the book written by the prophet Daniel. The opening verse of this story confirms that He is directing our quest for truth.

We read that Nebuchadnezzar the king made an image of gold, whose height was sixty cubits and its width six cubits. He set it up in the plain of Dura, in the province of Babylon.[18] This rebellious king, in defiance of the King of heaven, sets up an idol made of gold, whose dimensions match two of the numbers involved in this mystery, sixty and six. However, the number six hundred is not explicitly mentioned here.

The God of heaven has had to hide certain things within His Word so that those who are not willing to follow His truth will not destroy either the Bible or His followers. This is one such hidden matter. To you it has been given to know the mysteries of the kingdom of God, but to the rest it is given in parables, that seeing they may not see, and hearing they may not understand.[19]

To see this matter clearly, we must realize that this idol is a figure of a man erected by Nebuchadnezzar for his own edification and glory. He built this idol in direct contradiction to the prophecy that God had revealed to him in his dream, and which was related to him by our brother Daniel. You remember that Nebuchadnezzar had a dream in which he saw an idol made out of four different metals. Daniel explained that the different metals represented different kingdoms, and that although Nebuchadnezzar was the head of gold, the kingdom of Babylon would eventually fall and other kingdoms would arise after it.[20]

Ultimately, all earthly kingdoms will be destroyed by the Rock, when Jesus Christ comes to establish the kingdom of God. It is this prediction – the establishment of the everlasting kingdom of God – that the king of Babylon rebels against in defiance. The king of Babylon did not want his kingdom to fall, ever, and therefore he built his idol entirely of gold, symbolizing that his kingdom

---

18 Daniel 3:1
19 Luke 8:10

20 Daniel 2:38-45

600, 60, AND 6

Revelation 13:17, 18: ...and that no one may buy or sell except one who has the mark or the name of the beast, or the number of his name. Here is wisdom. Let him who has understanding calculate the number of the beast, for it is the number of a man: His number is six hundred and sixty-six.

Ezra 2:1,2,13: Now these are the people of the province who came back from the captivity, of those who had been carried away, whom Nebuchadnezzar the king of Babylon had carried away to Babylon, and who returned to Jerusalem and Judah, everyone to his own city. ...The number of the men of the people of Israel: ...the people of Adonikam, six hundred and sixty-six; ...

II Chronicles 9:13; I Kings 10:14: The weight of gold that came to Solomon yearly was six hundred and sixty-six talents of gold...

Where in the Bible do these verses point to understand this mystery?

King Nebuchadnezzar takes God's people captive (Ezra 2). He sets up an idol (Revelation 13), made from a lot of gold (I Kings and II Chronicles), and commands everyone to bow and worship this idol upon pain of death (Revelation 13). Everyone succumbs to the pressures of Babylon except a faithful few who trust God even unto death, and He delivers them (Ezra 2).

This is a description of history that is recorded in Daniel 3. This is history as prophecy.

The gold idol in Daniel 3 is set up in opposition to the vision in Daniel 2. God declares the fall of Babylon (Daniel 5) and this fall gives the framework to understand the biblical interpretation of the number and mark of the beast.

6 CUBITS
Mene = Measure
The width of the idol

60 CUBITS
Mene = Measure
The height of the idol

600 TALENTS /SHEKELS
Tekel = Weight
The weight of gold to build the Most Holy Place
Price in gold of the location of the temple

600,60,6 NUMBER OF THE BEAST
Peres = Divided/Fallen

BABYLON IS FALLEN!

would last forever. The God of heaven, the King of kings, has decreed the end from the beginning, and there is nothing that Nebuchadnezzar or any other earthly potentate can do against that Word. God declared that Babylon would fall, and of this we can be certain.

To deduce where the number six hundred might be in this story, we need to explain how this bold rebellion by the king of Babylon relates to the night that God executes judgment upon this pagan kingdom. The scene is depicted in the fifth chapter of the book of Daniel. On that night, Belshazzar, the descendant of king Nebuchadnezzar, sat upon the throne of Babylon hosting a drunken orgy for his government officials. While he was imbibing the wine of confusion from the sacred vessels taken out the sanctuary of God in Jerusalem, a bloodless hand appeared opposite the lampstand and wrote words like fire upon the wall. The king and his vassals were aroused from their drunken stupor and were struck with terror. As in the days of Nebuchadnezzar, none of the astrologers, necromancers, sorcerers, or Chaldeans could read or interpret the writing. Again the wise sage Daniel was called.

Our brother Daniel spoke the truth to the inebriated king, sparing nothing in his denunciations of the wickedness of the young monarch. He then read the words etched upon the walls of that blasphemous orgy.

Beloved, consider that in the Bible we only have three things expressly and directly written by God Himself. The Ten Commandments were written with the very finger of God;[21] we should earnestly pray that they should be written on our hearts and minds.[22] One time God wrote with His finger, yet we know not what He wrote: Jesus wrote the sins of some accusers in the sand before a woman taken in adultery.[23] And now here we see that God wrote a message for all humanity to read and understand.

---

21 Exodus 31:18; Deuteronomy 5:22
22 Hebrews 8:10
23 John 8:8, 9

All Scripture is given by inspiration of God,[24] and every word of God is pure.[25] Since this is true, how much more should we carefully study that which God Himself has written with His own hand in His Word.

The message engraved by the divine signature on the walls of the Babylonian palace was read by Daniel: *Mene, Mene, Tekel, Upharsin. Mene* literally means to number, to set, or to measure. *Tekel* literally means to weigh. *Upharsin* means to divide or split up. The judgment against the kingdom of confusion is declared by the writing on the wall.

You will remember that God revealed to Nebuchadnezzar in a dream the future of Babylon and its eventual fall through the idol of the multi-metal man. By contrast, the golden image of Babylon was set up in retaliation against the prophetic declaration of God that Babylon will fall. Nevertheless, the Word of God stands forever.[26]

The application of this writing to the prophecy for these last days reveals that God indeed knows the end from the beginning, and He can transform history into prophecy. *Mene:* measure, or number, the golden man that the king of Babylon set up. The height is sixty. Again, *Mene:* measure, or number, the golden image. The width is six. *Tekel:* weigh the image. The weight of the statue is not given in the story. Where could the king of Babylon have gotten so much gold to build a statue sixty cubits (ninety feet) high by six cubits (nine feet) wide?

Twice it is mentioned in Scripture that Solomon received six hundred sixty and six talents of gold annually when he reigned in Jerusalem.[27] God puts things in His Word twice when they are important. Doubtless the gold Nebuchadnezzar used in crafting his idolatrous symbol of defiance came from the precious metals taken as booty from Israel. More precisely, it would be logical for the king of confusion, in his insolence, to use the gold from the temple

---

24 *II Peter 1:21*
25 *Proverbs 30:5*
26 *Isaiah 40:8*

27 *I Kings 10:14; II Chronicles 9:13*

of God in constructing his self-glorifying image.

The plan of the king of Babylon was in direct opposition to what God had revealed to him as the truth of the future. He set up his so-called god on the plain of Dura in place of the God of Israel and His temple in Jerusalem. Therefore, we must focus on the location and the construction of the dwelling place of God on earth to further understand this mystery.

The location for the temple in Jerusalem was chosen by God. When King David sought to stay the plague inflicted upon the nation because of his sin of numbering the people, he was instructed to purchase the threshing floor of Ornan and offer sacrifice there.[28] This would later become the site of the temple constructed by Solomon on Mount Moriah.[29] And what was the purchase price of this location? By weight, six hundred shekels of gold.[30] Furthermore, when Solomon built the Most Holy Place inside the temple, the Bible records that a large amount of gold was required for its construction. How much gold was used in the Most Holy Place, the very dwelling place of God on earth? By weight, six hundred talents of gold.[31]

Although the Bible does not explicitly state the weight of the idol set up by the king of Babylon, it is clear that Nebuchadnezzar destroyed the temple of God in Jerusalem, including the Most Holy Place. Further, we know that the image that this rebellious king set up was in direct conflict with what the God of heaven had revealed to Nebuchadnezzar in his dream. The king of Babylon was trying to substitute the presence of the one true and living God with his inanimate idol of gold.

Elect of God, surely God has revealed the mystery of this number to us through His Word. The application of these numbers to this story then is: *Mene* (measure, number): the width of the idol is six. *Mene* (measure, number): the height of the idol is sixty. *Tekel* (weigh): the weight of the gold taken from the Most

---

28 *I Chronicles 21:18, 22*
29 *II Chronicles 3:1*
30 *I Chronicles 21:25*

31 *II Chronicles 3:8*

Holy Place to substitute the idol for the presence of God is six hundred. Six hundred sixty and six is the number of the man,[32] and the man is the idol set up to represent and glorify the king of Babylon, the regent of confusion on this earth. Here is the man, the king of spiritual Babylon, who will enforce the mark of allegiance to rebellion against God.

Let us look in detail at the story of the golden idol set up by the king of Babylon. This story contains several other important parallels that we need to study. The devil creates a very subtle counterfeit that opposes what God is doing in these last days.

God has a particular message to be given right before the return of Jesus to take His ransomed saints to the kingdom: it is the message of the three angels mentioned in the previous chapter. It should not surprise us that the devil would craft a devious, conflicting message to try to counteract the power of the final warning message given by God. We find such a message

of deception and fear in this story written by Daniel, and it is through this story that we will see what the mark of the beast is and how people will receive it. We will also see that what is contained within the Most Holy Place of the temple of God is the key to completing the understanding of the prophetic puzzle surrounding the son of Satan and his mark.

In the final warning message given by God, the first angel comes having the everlasting gospel to preach to those who dwell on the earth—to every nation, tribe, tongue, and people.[33]

In the counterfeit call to worship issued by Satan, a herald cries aloud, commanding all peoples, nations, and languages to participate in the veneration of the idol.[34] Both messages are for all peoples, in all tongues, throughout the earth.

The message of the first angel from heaven is, Fear God and give glory to Him, for the hour of His judgment has come; and worship Him who made

---

32 Revelation 13:18

33 Revelation 14:6
34 Daniel 3:4

heaven and earth, the sea and springs of water.[35] All creatures are called to honor the one true Creator God, and to worship Him in the manner that He has commanded. It is the time of judgment, just prior to the return of the Son of God.

The apostate power sends out its command, saying that at the time of the playing of the sound of the horn, flute, harp, lyre, psaltery, dulcimer in symphony with all kinds of music, all must fall down and worship the gold image that King Nebuchadnezzar has set up.[36] This is a command that is a direct insult to the God of heaven. Instead of worshipping the Creator, this man claims the adoration of the deity and orders all to worship the created object. The king exchanges the truth of God for the lie, and demands that man worship and serve the creature rather than the Creator, who is blessed forever.[37] When the threat of death invoking false worship is given, it represents the closing of the time of judgment.

The second angel comes from heaven with a strong warning, denouncing all forms of false worship, crying out, Babylon is fallen, is fallen, that great city, because she has made all nations drink of the wine of the wrath of her fornication.[38] The wine Babylon causes all nations to drink is her confusing teachings, and while men are intoxicated with these falsehoods, they commit spiritual fornication with this whore of a religion by uniting the material interests of the government together with that of the apostate faith. She is fallen into sin and every form of deception, and the God of heaven will soon cause her to suffer for her blasphemy.

When we read the story of the golden idol of Babylon in the Holy Scriptures, it appears as if there is no direct parallel, yet contradictory, message to the second angel's message of God. However, dear brethren, if we look at the main object of contention in the story, we find that the counterfeit message is staring us in the face. The idol standing sixty cubits (90 feet) high and six cubits (9 feet) wide, made of gold taken from the

---

35 *Revelation 14:7*
36 *Daniel 3:5*
37 *Romans 1:25*

38 *Revelation 14:8*

sanctuary of God, is itself the second false message from Satan. The God of heaven declared what would be in the future by giving a dream of a multi-metal man to Nebuchadnezzar. God declared that Babylon, the head of gold, will fall and be replaced by other kingdoms. Eventually, all of these other earthly kingdoms will be overturned by the kingdom of God. Yet in an affront to God, the king of Babylon seeks to usurp His prerogatives and orders that an image made entirely of gold be set up. In essence the king defies God with his statue and declares: Babylon is not fallen, and will never fall! Instead, the king of Babylon commands that everyone else fall: fall down and worship his golden idol.

The third angel's message contains the most direct, ominous warning given in the entire Bible. If anyone worships the beast and his image, and receives his mark on his forehead or on his hand, he himself shall also drink of the wine of the wrath of God, which is poured out full strength into the cup of His indignation. He shall be tormented with fire and brimstone in the presence of the holy angels and in the presence of the Lamb. And the smoke of their torment ascends forever and ever; and they have no rest day or night, who worship the beast and his image, and whoever receives the mark of his name. Here is the patience of the saints; here are those who keep the commandments of God and the faith of Jesus.[39]

The king of Babylon, acting as the vice-regent of Satan on earth, has his own threat to make in contrast with the third angel's message of God. He boastfully proclaims, You shall fall down and worship the gold image that King Nebuchadnezzar has set up; and whoever does not fall down and worship shall be cast immediately into the midst of a burning fiery furnace.[40]

Beloved, we stand on the verge of eternity. Soon all will have to choose: serve the living God, the Maker of heaven and earth, or serve Satan and his idolatrous systems of worship. Those who worship God may be persecuted and tormented for their faith,

---

39 *Revelation 14:9-12*
40 *Daniel 3:5, 6*

but they will inherit eternal life. Those who follow the prince of darkness will be destroyed in the fires of hell.

Now therefore, fear the Lord, serve Him in sincerity and in truth, and put away all false gods. Serve the Lord! And if it seems evil to you to serve the Lord, choose for yourselves this day whom you will serve, whether the Creator of heaven, earth, the seas and fountains of waters, or the false gods of Babylon. But as for me and my house, we will serve the Lord.[41]

The key to understanding the contrast between the two messages is the concluding phrase shared by the third angel messenger of God: Here is the patience of the saints; here are those who keep the commandments of God and the faith of Jesus.[42] The Commandments of God reveal who we truly worship, for it was our Savior Jesus who said that if we love Him, we will keep His Commandments.[43]

Beloved, we reasoned that the king of Babylon secured the gold for the idol from the temple in Jerusalem, and in particular, from the Most Holy Place. Within the veil of the Most Holy Place there was only one object, the Ark of the Covenant covered by the Mercy Seat.[44] Within the Ark were the Ten Commandments written by the finger of God.

The king of Babylon, in erecting his golden idol, seeks to not only destroy the dwelling place of God and usurp the throne of God as did Satan, but he also tries to do away with the law of God and cause man to transgress that which is holy, and just, and good.[45]

Of the Ten Commandments, the first four relate to worship. Let us consider these commandments in light of this history about false worship and understand how it relates to its prophetic fulfillment today.

The first commandment is: I am the Lord your God, who brought you out of the land of Egypt, out of the house of bondage. You shall have no other gods

---

41 *Joshua 24:14, 15*
42 *Revelation 14:12*
43 *John 14:15*

44 *Exodus 26:33, 34*
45 *Romans 7:12*

before Me.[46] Anyone who bows down in obeisance to the image of the king of Babylon is placing another god before the God of heaven. This is sin.

The second commandment is: You shall not make for yourself a carved image, or any likeness of anything that is in heaven above, or that is in the earth beneath, or that is in the water under the earth; you shall not bow down to them nor serve them. For I, the Lord your God, am a jealous God, visiting the iniquity of the fathers on the children to the third and fourth generations of those who hate Me, but showing mercy to thousands, to those who love Me and keep My commandments.[47] Clearly, anyone who is giving reverence to a created object is not worshipping the Creator who made the heavens, the earth, and the water. This is sin.

The third commandment is: You shall not take the name of the Lord your God in vain, for the Lord will not hold him guiltless who takes His name in vain.[48] You who are true believers understand that you cannot claim to be a Christian with your voice, and then turn around and deny the God who redeemed you with His blood by your actions, for it is hypocrisy. This is sin.

The fourth commandment reads: Remember the Sabbath day, to keep it holy. Six days you shall labor and do all your work, but the seventh day is the Sabbath of the Lord your God. In it you shall do no work: you, nor your son, nor your daughter, nor your male servant, nor your female servant, nor your cattle, nor your stranger who is within your gates. For in six days the Lord made the heavens and the earth, the sea, and all that is in them, and rested the seventh day. Therefore the Lord blessed the Sabbath day and hallowed it.[49]

The Sabbath commandment very distinctly identifies who our God is: He is our Creator and Redeemer. We demonstrate our love and loyalty to Him by keeping holy the day that He ordains and declares to

---

46 *Exodus 20:2, 3; Deuteronomy 5:6, 7*
47 *Exodus 20:4-6;*
   Deuteronomy 5:8-10

48 *Exodus 20:7; Deuteronomy 5:11*
49 *Exodus 20:8-11;*
   Deuteronomy 5:12-15

be holy. This is not, as some would erroneously suggest, legalism. Nay, rather, it is a weekly joyful testimony of our faith. In observing the seventh-day Sabbath commandment, we illustrate our faith that we believe the Bible, that God means what He says, and that God and God alone is able to bless a day and set it apart as holy.

The seventh-day is from sundown on Friday evening until sundown Saturday night. It is the only day that the Bible declares God sanctified and blessed. Keeping holy the day that God ordained and blessed is an act of faith.

Beloved, I know that many of you were raised believing that the Sabbath was changed to Sunday. This is an error that the son of Satan has sought to perpetuate in turning people away from the God of heaven. Over five hundred years before the establishment of the papacy, our brother Daniel foresaw this malicious attempt to deceive when he was given the vision of the little horn power that would think to change times and laws.[50]

Those who bow down and worship the idol set up by the monarch of Babylon do not adhere to the Sabbath of the Lord God of the Bible. They follow their inclinations and political aspirations at the expense of their soul.

By ignoring the Sabbath of the Lord, they neglect the Lord of the Sabbath, Jesus Christ.[51] In the day when He shall return on the clouds of heaven, Christ shall declare to such willfully rebellious false disciples, I never knew you; depart from Me, you who practice lawlessness![52]

Worship is the final issue at the end of time. Satan has sought to cause all to worship him instead of the one true Creator and Redeemer God, Jesus Christ. God gives explicit instructions in His Word about how we are to worship Him. When we choose to ignore His commands, and worship in the way established by man instead of God, we are actually worshipping ourselves. That is

---

50 *Daniel 7:25*
51 *Mark 2:27, 28*
52 *Matthew 7:23*

what Satan did in heaven. That was the first sin, and it remains the most common and the most dreadful sin in the universe: pride. Pride is most indignantly manifested in setting oneself above the Word of God, above God Himself.

Returning to the story of the golden image of Nebuchadnezzar, we learn additional information that relates to the image that will be set up in the last days. The king of Babylon called together all the government officials in his realm to this religious ceremony. Here is a classic example of spiritual fornication: the manipulation and use of the power of the state to enforce religious dogma.

The order is given that all must bow down to this golden idol when the entertainment from Babylon begins. Beloved, I submit to you that many, many even of the elect, are being desensitized to bow before idols through the Babylonian entertainment of our day: music that stimulates immoral activity, television programs and movies

that promote violence and sexual depravity, and computer programs and internet sites that urge the base passions of animals upon the human mind. I charge you, dear friends: Do not be deceived, God is not mocked; for whatever a man sows, that he will also reap. For he who sows to his flesh will of the flesh reap corruption, but he who sows to the Spirit will of the Spirit reap everlasting life.[53]

If you are not disgusted by the brazen acts of iniquity that are flashed across your mind through the media, then you need to be concerned. You may be desensitized to truth and righteousness. I appeal to you to recognize that if you are bowing to these images on your stereos, televisions and computer screens now, your character is being subconsciously weakened to prepare you to succumb to the temptation to bow before the golden idol of Satan.

All across the plains of Dura in Babylon knees bend and heads bow. Thousands are gathered there, and all submit to the decree of the confused despot;

_____
53 *Galatians 6:7*

all except three emasculated Hebrew prisoners of war.[54] These three stood the test of appetite with Daniel when faced with the temptation of having to eat unclean foods and things offered to idols.[55] They stood the test then; they will stand the test now.

Who are these young men that would dare defy the ruler of this world? The names of these three young men help to explain why they could stand while the others fell down prostrate before the idol.

Throughout the Bible a name was given to a person to reflect his character. In some instances the name was changed following a momentous occasion.

The meaning of the name of God is a reflection of His character. God proclaimed His name to Moses as: The Lord, the Lord God, merciful and gracious, longsuffering, and abounding in goodness and truth, keeping mercy for thousands, forgiving iniquity and transgression and sin, by no means clearing the guilty, visiting the iniquity of the fathers upon the children and the children's children to the third and the fourth generation.[56] It is this name of God – His character - which will be written upon the foreheads [minds] of those who stand up against the satanic trinity in these last days.[57]

Examples of the meaning of names include Jacob, the deceiver, whose name was changed to Israel, prince with God, after his night of wrestling in prayer.[58] The names of each of the twelve tribes of Israel are full of meaning. These include Judah (praise),[59] and Asher (happiness).[60] The most wonderful name given among men was told to Joseph and Mary by an angel: you shall call His name Jesus, for He will save His people from their sins.[61] The name Jesus literally means, God saves, or Savior.

Although the Babylonian king changed the names of the three faithful witnesses of the

---

54 *Isaiah 39:5-7*
55 *Daniel 1:6-16*
56 *Exodus 34:6, 7*
57 *Revelation 14:1*
58 *Genesis 32:27, 28*
59 *Genesis 29:35*
60 *Genesis 30:13*
61 *Matthew 1:21*

God of heaven to reflect the names of the deities of Chaldea (Shadrach, Meshach, and Abed-Nego),[62] he could not change their character. Their Hebrew names and characters are: Hananiah, whose name means, The Lord has been gracious; Mishael, which means, Who is what God is; and Azariah, who is, The Lord has helped.

Some people have inquired about Daniel in this story. Where was Daniel at the time that the golden idol rose up as all the leaders of the then known world bowed down? Surely he would have had to be present for this dramatic event as he had recently been promoted to serve in the court of the king.[63] Fellow believers, I believe that the question should not be where was Daniel? but, why was Daniel not present? on that fateful afternoon. There are two reasons.

What's in a name? As we have seen, much in every way. Daniel is an appropriate name, for it means, The Lord is my judge.

When the golden idol is lifted up, and all are commanded to bow under threat of capital punishment, Daniel is not present because the time for judgment has passed. Everyone has already made their decision. Those who will take a stand against the enforcement of idolatrous worship have been making their decision daily, and their characters are formed for eternity. It will be said in that day: He who is unjust, let him be unjust still; he who is filthy, let him be filthy still; he who is righteous, let him be righteous still; he who is holy, let him be holy still.[64] Judgment is over at the time that the golden idol is set up, and therefore, The Lord is my Judge – Daniel – is not present.

The other reason that Daniel was not there at this occasion commemorating rebellion is that he was not supposed to be there. At the last hour of earth's history, when those controlled by the unholy spirit erect a golden image to the son of Satan, there are only

---

62 Daniel 1:7
63 Daniel 2:48

64 Revelation 22:11

three angel messengers sent to oppose this blasphemous work. Hananiah, Mishael, and Azariah represent those who live in our day and stand up against this culminating act of Satan to cause people to worship him. The fourth messenger who gives strength and power to the final warning message is the Lord Jesus Christ through His Spirit calling, Come out of her, My people.[65]

The three messengers of God are faithful under trial. When pressured to bow to the idol or be thrown into a fiery furnace, they stand for the Word of God. Their response to the fury of the king should echo in our hearts as we prepare for a similar experience: We have no need to answer you in this matter. If that is the case, our God whom we serve is able to deliver us from the burning fiery furnace, and He will deliver us from your hand, O king. But if not, let it be known to you, O king, that we do not serve your gods, nor will we worship the gold image which you have set up.[66]

With this hopeful declaration of faith, the king of confusion is enraged. He orders that the fire be heated seven times hotter.[67] Yet I want you to understand, dear beloved, whose Hand is on the thermostat. In Scripture seven is the perfect number. The color of perfect fire is pure white. Christ had control over the dimensions of the golden idol; He has control over the fires of affliction that shall befall us. It is for this reason that Jesus declares concerning some of us that we will walk with Him in white, for we will be worthy.[68]

The king of this world will seek to bind up the three angels' messengers, even as the king of Babylon bound up the three captives to cast them into the fire. However, the three faithful are covered from head to toe before being thrown into what was expected to become their crematorium.[69] Even so, beloved, those who go forth to proclaim the three angels' messages for this last hour must be completely clad in the righteousness of Jesus.[70] The

---

65 Revelation 18:4
66 Daniel 3:16-18

67 Daniel 3:19
68 Revelation 3:4
69 Daniel 3:21
70 Isaiah 61:10

king of Babylon, infuriated in a demonic frenzy brought on by his idolatry,[71] hurled the three sentinels of God into the furnace and the flames consumed their would be assassins.[72] The Bible records that as the three men entered the oven of execution, they fell down bound into the midst of the burning fiery furnace.[73] Elect of God, these three trustworthy messengers did not merely stumble into the furnace. No, no, never!

Six times the command of the king of Babylon to fall before the golden image to Satan is repeated in this story; six times the three messengers of God remained loyal to the Creator of the heavens, earth, seas and fountains of water, and refused to bow down to the idol. Now that they are in the furnace, however, they have every reason to bow down and worship. The Son of God is waiting amidst the flames of affliction to protect them and walk with them in their trials.[74]

This story is very representative of the contrast between the service of Satan and the worship of the God of heaven. Satan orders all to come before him and bow down or else be killed. On the other hand, when we are broken and bowed down with affliction, in some cases seemingly to the point of death, Jesus picks us up, heals us, and walks with us in our trials.

O beloved, our Savior calls us to take our Christianity seriously, to awaken out of the spiritual lethargy that we have bought into because of the commercialism and materialism among the flock of God. It is my prayer that the genuineness of your faith, being much more precious than gold that perishes, though it is tested by fire, may be found to praise, honor, and glory at the revelation of Jesus Christ, whom having not seen you love. Though now you do not see Him, yet believing, you rejoice with joy inexpressible and full of glory, receiving the end of your faith—the salvation of your souls.[75]

---

71 I Corinthians 10:19, 20
72 Daniel 3:22
73 Daniel 3:23
74 Daniel 3:25

75 I Peter 1:7-9

At the time that the idolatrous symbol of confusion and rebellion is set up in homage to the king of spiritual Babylon, those who have put their trust in the Lamb of God and have sought to obey His word will have characters that reflect those who were thrown in the flames of persecution centuries earlier. Remember that the name represents the character. Therefore, we will praise our loving Savior because He has transformed our characters. We will declare that the Lord has been gracious, the Lord has helped, and our hearts and minds reveal that we are in character what God is in character. These are the meanings of the names of Hananiah, Azariah, Mishael, the three messengers who stood for Christ in the midst of Babylon and walked with Jesus in the flames.

Our compassionate Savior loves us and gave His life for us. He has a deep longing in His heart for the people who live at the very end of time, the church of the Laodiceans. He knows the end from the beginning, and He knows the fiery trials that await His people in these last days. He pleads with us: I counsel you to buy from Me gold refined in the fire, that you may be rich and white garments, that you may be clothed, that the shame of your nakedness may not be revealed. As many as I love, I rebuke and chasten.[76]

---

76 Revelation 3:18, 19

Chapter Nine

YOU SHALL COME FORTH AS GOLD

My beloved and longed-for brethren, my joy and crown, stand fast in the Lord. The Lord is at hand. The things which you learn and receive and hear from the Scriptures, these do, and the God of peace will be with you.[1]

Brethren, I realize that much of what has been shared is difficult to understand and challenging to accept. Yet the Word of God is true. Although we may be startled to realize the extent of the deception perpetrated against man by our spiritual enemy, we should be thankful that God reveals these things in His Word. Therefore, as you wrestle with some of the issues raised in what has been shared here, I urge you to be anxious for nothing, but in everything by prayer and supplication, with thanksgiving, let your requests be made known to God; and the peace of God, which surpasses all understanding, will guard your hearts and minds through Christ Jesus.[2]

The Bible makes it clear that at the end of time, a Satanic trinity will exist that will cause all, both small and great, rich and poor, free and slave, to receive a mark on their right hand or on their foreheads, and that no one may buy or sell except one who has the mark or the name of the beast, or the number of his name.[3]

Those controlled by the unholy spirit set up an image to the son of Satan and force all men to worship his image. In so doing, all who give obeisance to this idolatrous command are actually worshipping the dragon, Satan. Let us be perfectly clear about what is meant by these symbols.

The Bible clearly identifies the dragon as that serpent of old, called the Devil and Satan, who

---

1 *Philippians 4:1, 5, 9*

2 *Philippians 4:6, 7*
3 *Revelation 13:17*

deceives the whole world.[4] Of this there should be no doubt.

That the beast who resembles the dragon is the son of Satan should also be without question. Moreover, based on the characteristics given in the Bible, it is abundantly clear that the son of Satan is the Papacy, the system of the Roman Catholic Church. It is the only power that matches the criteria of the beast described so clearly in the books of Daniel and Revelation. Just as with the kingdoms of Babylon, Medo-Persia, Greece, and pagan Rome, the Roman Catholic Church is a religious power that seduces with the powers of government in a form of spiritual fornication in order to advance its own inerests. In the process, it frequently and ruthlessly persecutes the people of God. Yea, the son of Satan is indeed like his father, the devil, who was a murderer from the beginning, and is the father of lies.[5]

The other beast of the hellish trinity has two horns like a lamb, but speaks like Satan, the dragon. This is the unholy spirit, also known as the false prophet.[6] Scripture identifies this beast as a spiritualistic movement in which people actively communicate with and are controlled by spirit beings. This is a masterfully crafted deception in which Satan snares people in apostate religious groups which reject the plain testimony of the Word of God, and accept the lies and delusions of unclean spirits. This is manifested in those religious gatherings where a spirit of confusion is present and people babble all sorts of nonsense and claim that it is a gift from God. Other deceptive practices may be present in such assemblies, including the supposed power to heal, cast out demons, and other such miracles, yet the source of the power is not of heaven. This is the spiritual aspect of the beast that rises out of the earth.

But what of the political side of this beast? As with all the other beasts we have seen, the religious powers unite with, or manipulate for their own purposes, the powers of the state. In this way Satan works

---

4 Revelation 12:9
5 John 8:44

6 Revelation 16:13

through religious and political institutions to oppose the work of God and His people.

We saw that the amalgamated beast, which is the son of Satan, arose out of the sea. The Bible tells us that the sea is a symbol for peoples, multitudes, nations, and tongues.[7] By contrast, the beast that is controlled by the unholy spirit rises from the earth,[8] not from the sea. This implies that this beast that speaks as a dragon came not from a place of many peoples, but from a land relatively uninhabited.

We also saw that just as the Holy Spirit was not poured out with great power until the time appointed for it, on the Day of Pentecost, so too this unholy spirit did not begin to manifest itself until after the deadly wound of the son of Satan was inflicted. This occurred in 1798 when the Pope was dethroned. Only after this time could the next significant geo-political empire arise from the earth.

This beast tells those who dwell on the earth to make an image to the beast who was wounded by the sword and lived.[9] From these words we understand that the religious bodies themselves would not directly erect the image to the son of Satan. Instead, they would work through the political powers, instructing the people of the earth in a democratic process, to erect this monument to the son of Satan. It will be the people themselves who are responsible for establishing this object of desecration and choosing to align themselves with the prince of darkness.

Consider what nation or government was coming up from an uninhabited area some time following 1798, to be ruled by the people, of the people, and for the people. This beast-like nation would look like a lamb, yet speak as a dragon, and would grow into the next world's superpower. Plainly we see that Bible identifies the political aspect of this beast to be the United States of America.

When the powers of the fallen, apostate churches in the United States unite with

---

7 *Revelation 17:15*
8 *Revelation 13:11*

9 *Revelation 13:14*

the government to enforce laws against the principles of freedom of conscience, then this unholy spirit beast will be ready to persecute, maim, and destroy those who oppose its false doctrines. Very soon we will see the forces of the unholy spirit – fallen churches filled with demons and false doctrines – manipulate the power of the government of the United States of America, leading the people of the world to erect an image to the son of Satan. Indeed, based on the recent political history of the USA, it can be argued that this prophecy is being fulfilled in our day.

Why, you may ask, would the government of the United States of America and the apostate Protestant churches unite to create an object of worship that gives glory to the Papacy? Two very simple and very common reasons: money and power.

The love of money is a root of all kinds of evil, for which some have strayed from the faith in their greediness, and pierced themselves through with many sorrows.[10] Look at what happened to the Roman Catholic Church in her quest for power and profit. To see just how far she has strayed from the simplicity of the gospel, compare the lives of the leaders of the two systems, the true and the false, Jesus Christ and the Pope.

Although Jesus was rich, yet for our sakes He became poor.[11] Truly it can be said of the humble Carpenter of Nazareth that His kingdom was not of this world.[12] Lovely Jesus, our Savior and King, freely offers forgiveness through His blood to anyone who comes to Him with a penitent heart.

By contrast, the Roman Catholic Church is the richest kingdom on earth. Boasting adherents and owning real estate in more countries of the world than any other nation, yet it occupies the smallest parcel of land of any independent country. Do not think that the Catholic Church, who ruled this world for over twelve hundred years, suddenly became financially bankrupt when the deadly wound was struck at the turn of the 19th century. Hardly. And how did she amass such wealth? She did

---

10 I Timothy 6:10

11 II Corinthians 8:9
12 John 18:36

it in part by claiming to be able to sell pardon for sin through the price of an indulgence, and by keeping people bound by superstitious fears.

Beloved, do not be misled by external appearances. Which country is the poorest nation on the face of the planet? Or, put another way, which country owes more money than any other nation in the world? The United States of America. No other peoples are even close to the level of indebtedness, individually and collectively, to that of the USA.

Common sense tells us that if there is a borrower, there must also be a lender. Yet what country could ever afford to lend the trillions of dollars necessary to feed the insatiable appetite of covetousness that reigns in America? Consider the reality of the global economy. The continents of Africa, South America and Australia combined could not make a dent in supplying the financial resources demanded by the people of the United States. The powers of Asia are just now beginning to

amass wealth, and that, too, only as fast as the Americans will spend. The European economies have a history of wealth, but not sufficient to feed the unquenchable cravings for more debt by the United States. There is only one power that has the resources to make that level of financial commitment. Only the beast who for over a millennium ruled this planet by the sword, the rack and the stake has the financial resources hidden away to satisfy these cravings.

The borrower is servant to the lender.[13] This is easily seen in the way that the United States treats the Roman Catholic Church, and especially its primary dignitary, the Pope. Whenever a foreign dignitary comes to visit the President of America, whether they are from Germany, Japan, the United Kingdom, or any other country, the leader of the foreign nation meets the President at the White House. However, when the Pope flies into the United States, the President is there to receive him at the airport. This is diplomatic protocol: the less powerful goes to

---

13 Proverbs 22:7

where the more powerful is to receive him.

Recently there was a museum dedicated to Pope John Paul II opened in Washington, D.C., the capital of the United States of America. Although the Pope himself did not attend the ceremonies inaugurating the new facility, he arranged for his vassal, the President of the United States of America, to preside over the opening of the museum. Increasingly, when officials from the United States attend an international conference on family issues, the delegation backs the policies propagated by the son of Satan. Amazingly, at the funeral of the most recently deceased Pope, three US presidents knelt before his open casket, the first time any US head of state has attended such a function in the Vatican. When the newest pope comes to visit the US, the President goes to meet him at the airport, he is given a birthday party attended by over 10,000 at the White House, and he is given the floor of the United Nations as a pulpit. Why? Power and money. All the world marvels and follows the beast.[14]

How does this affect the Protestant religion? The fallen churches in America are alarmed at the decline in morality of their country. These churches are not willing to deal with the root cause of the problem: sin, which is the transgression of the law.[15] The churches have abandoned the Word of God, supplanted the law of God with the traditions of men, and are feeding the flock with psycho-babble and infotainment that lulls the people into a spiritual sleep. Moral relativism now prevails in most churches because they have rejected the law of God. Some of these bodies are actually willing to allow homosexuals to become shepherds of the flock. Pity the poor congregations that will not follow the Word of God forbidding this abomination.[16] Jesus cries out, Come out of her, My people.[17]

---

14 Revelation 13:3
15 I John 3:4
16 Lev. 18:22, 20:13; Rom. 1:24-27;
    I Cor. 6:9; I Tim. 1:9, 10
17 Revelation 18:4

These churches cannot effect a change in society through spiritual revival – because they themselves have fallen into spiritual fornication – and so they seek to advance their agenda through political measures.

Fellow churchgoers, let no one misinform you: morality cannot be legislated. If the law of God cannot save you, how much less can the opinions and traditions of men rescue society from sliding into the moral abyss? Only Jesus Christ can transform the heart – one person at a time. Churches should be preaching the gospel of the cross instead of allowing the pulpit to become a distribution center for politically correct voter cards.

Our brothers and sisters who held onto the pure faith of the Word of God often had to surrender their lives rather than bow to the insolent demands of the son of Satan, the Papacy. Yet what do we see in the majority of the churches outside of the Roman Catholic fold in our

day? They are apologizing to the great apostate for having ever protested against what are now considered minor theological differences. People were once burned at the stake for not participating in the blasphemous mass of Catholicism. Others who would not bow down to idols were tortured so badly that death was a sweet relief. And today's Christian leaders call these minor theological differences! What startling spiritual indifference!

Martin Luther boldly stood before the antichristian power and declared him to be the very offspring of Satan. Since the time of Luther the Papacy has descended lower and lower into confusion and rebellion, with the Pope going so far as to claim infallibility. The Catholic Church still teaches that salvation comes through the ministry of the sacraments and works. The Bible declares that salvation is by grace through faith alone.[18] Idolatry abounds in every Catholic sanctuary, and invoking the favor of Mary

---

18 *Ephesians 2:8*

and other dead saints persists in this harlot of a religion.

As the unholy spirit takes possession of the former Protestant churches, they are drawn steadily further into the snare laid for them by Satan. The fallen churches are unwittingly running back to the fold of the Papacy in order to gain political power. At the same time, the United States of America as a nation is grossly indebted to the Roman Catholic Church. This indebtedness is not publicly disclosed, yet can be understood simply by perusing the global economic scene. Holding companies can be established with clandestine links so that the source of the original funding can never be made. Funds can furtively be transferred in and out of the banks of Switzerland, the country which supplies the guards for the Papacy. The Swiss banking system is totally secretive.

Soon shall these churches, uniting with the powers of the indebted government powers, raise up the image to the Papacy as prophesied.[19]

The worship of the golden image erected by the literal king of Babylon involved the transgression of the four commandments given to man governing the worship of God. The image to be set up in these last days in honor of the head of spiritual Babylon will also force all, under threat of death, to transgress the commandments of God that deal with worship. The special object of desecration by Satan and his demonic trinity concerns those commandments that specifically set the God of heaven apart from all other so-called gods. There are two such commandments, but it is only necessary for the king of confusion to try to alter one in order to break all the others.[20] It should not be surprising that Satan, through his vicar, the Papacy, would attack the one commandment that requires more faith to believe than any other.

The fourth commandment of God begins with the word, Remember.[21] Yet there can be little doubt that most of the Christian church has forgotten this command God wrote indelibly with His own hand on

19 Revelation 13:14-18

20 James 2:10
21 Exodus 20:8

TWO SYSTEMS OF WORSHIP

2 FAMILIES
The family of God (Father, Son, and Holy Spirit).

The family of Satan (Satan, the Papacy, Spiritualism).

2 LAST DAY MESSAGES
Worship the Creator; Judgment is Now; Babylon is fallen; If you accept the mark of the beast you will perish because of your sins.

Worship the Creature; Judgment is Now; Babylon will never fall; If you do not accept the mark of the beast, you will be killed.

2 LEADERS
Jesus Christ who gave His life for our salvation.

The Papacy who kills those who do not follow his traditions.

2 DAYS OF WORSHIP
The holy seventh-day Sabbath of our Creator and Saviour Jesus Christ.

The pagan day of the sun set up by Satan.

tables of stone, and by His Holy Spirit, on our hearts.

In remembering the seventh-day Sabbath [Saturday] to keep it holy, we remember our Creator and the One who brought us out from the bondage of sin and unbelief. The seventh-day Sabbath is the only day that God set apart as holy and sanctified, and He invites us to spend this day with Him, that we might be sanctified by Him. The Sabbath is the special sign that it is He that is restoring His image in us and not we ourselves.[22] Far too often, it appears as if contemporary Christians seek to recreate God in their own image, rather than the other way around. Is it not because these churches have become a dwelling place of demons, a prison for every foul spirit, and a cage for every unclean and hated bird![23]

The devil has particular enmity for the Sabbath commandment. Those who love God with all their hearts and worship Him as He commands are no longer captive to the devil. We are changed from glory into glory by the indwelling Holy Spirit,[24] and we have special blessings promised from the Lord of the Universe when we meet with Him on the seventh-day Sabbath.[25]

The most subtle and successful of deceptions that Satan has perpetrated upon man at the expense of God is his claim, through his son, the Papacy, to have changed the day of rest from the seventh day to the first day of the week. The first day of the week is not holy; it is not blessed of God. The keeping of this day as a commemoration of religious importance is an invention of Satan to get people to worship him.

We saw that in the beginning Satan had a different name, Lucifer, which means the Morning Star. Brothers and sisters, there is only one star that comes out in the morning: the sun. Ever since he fell from heaven and became the Accuser, Lucifer has sought to pervert the worship of God so that man might turn

---

22 Ezekiel 20:12, 20
23 Revelation 18:3

24 II Corinthians 3:18
25 Genesis 2:3

their affections to him. In his efforts to cause man to forget the seventh-day Sabbath of God, and substituting in its place the observance of the first day of the week, the day of the sun, he accomplishes his goal.

Lucifer succeeds in enticing people to worship him by using the other members of his perverse trio. The confusion caused by the unholy spirit leads people to unite with the son of Satan, and in his honor they mandate the day of the sun as an object of worship. Nowhere does the Bible mention that Sunday is a holy, sacred or blessed day. Indeed, unlike the seventh-day Sabbath, the word Sunday does not even appear in the Bible. It is always only referred to as the first day of the week. Those who knowingly continue to follow the practice of worshipping on Sunday, in defiance of the commandment of God, are actually transgressing all four of the commandments that relate to the worship of the Lord God Almighty.

The God of heaven brought us out of the slavery of sin, and he requires that we worship none other.[26] Those who reject His Sabbath are rejecting Him. This breaks the first commandment. This is sin.

To knowingly follow this spurious holiday established to venerate the sun is to set up an idol in your heart that opposes the God who loves you, made you, and gave His life for you. Therefore, keeping Sunday as a rest day, in defiance of what God ordained, breaks the second commandment.[27] It is sin.

Those who reject the holy day of rest ordained by the God of heaven, the seventh-day Sabbath, and substitute in its place a pagan day honoring the golden globe orbiting in space, take the name of God in vain.[28] You cannot claim to be a Christian and worship the inventions of man. This breaks the third commandment. This is sin.

Several times in the Bible God told His people to place His

---

26 Exodus 20:2,3; Deuteronomy 5:6,7
27 Exodus 20:4-6;
    Deuteronomy 5:8-10
28 Exodus 20:7; Deuteronomy 5:11

law on their right hand and on their forehead.[29] Rather than wearing a phylactery, God wants to write His law on our hearts and in our minds,[30] so that whatever we do with our hands, or think in our hearts, will be consistent with the law of God.[31] Beloved, understand that the seal of God which is placed upon the forehead of His people is His name, His character, and His law. The sign that we have been sealed by the Holy Spirit,[32] the seal of our sanctification by God,[33] is the obedient observance of the seventh-day Sabbath (Saturday) of the Creator.[34]

Conversely, Satan seeks to counterfeit the seal of God with his own mark. In the last moments of time, the unholy spirit beast will create a global movement dedicated to promoting this counterfeit day of rest in honor of the son of Satan. The powers of the nations will unite with the religious authorities to crush out any opposition to their specious holiday. This is the mark of allegiance to the powers of darkness. The setting up of the Sunday as a required day of worship, and the enforcement of this bogus holiday by the powers of the state around the world, is the mark of the beast.

Again, let us be perfectly clear. The dragon is Satan.[35] The amalgamated beast is the son of Satan, which is the Roman Catholic Church headed by the Pope.[36] The beast that looks like a lamb, but speaks as a dragon, is the unholy spirit of Satan. This represents the uniting of the powers of spiritualism with the churches that have replaced the Word of God with tradition and human theories, and have thereby become full of demons. These fallen churches then unite with the government, particularly the last global superpower, the United States of America, causing them to enact legislation that violates the conscience. The mark of the beast is the enforced observance of Sunday as a day

29 Exodus 13:9, 16; Deuteronomy 6:8; 11:18.
30 Jeremiah 31:31-33; Hebrews 8:8-12
31 Matthew 15:18
32 Ephesians 4:30
33 Ezekiel 20:12,20
34 Exodus 20:8-11

35 Revelation 12:9
36 Revelation 13:1-10

of worship. The number 600, 60, and 6, refers to the image set up representing the man who is at the head of spiritual Babylon, the Pope. To have his name is to have his character, which is that of antichrist,[37] the son of lawlessness.[38] Those who follow him worship his father, Satan.

In the very last moments of time, there will only be two classes of people alive on earth: those with vacillating characters who bow before the golden image to the sun, and those whose characters shine with the golden brightness of the faith and love of Jesus in obedience to His commands. But He knows the way that you take; when He has tested you, you shall come forth as gold.[39]

---

37 I John 2:18, 19
38 II Thessalonians 2:3,4
39 Job 23:10

Chapter Ten

IT IS DONE!

Elect according to the Word of God, we can do nothing against the truth, but for the truth. Become complete. Be of good comfort, be of one mind, live in peace; and the God of love and peace will be with you. The grace of the Lord Jesus Christ, and the love of God, and the communion of the Holy Spirit be with you all.[1]

Beloved, do not be disturbed by the things that I share with you, for they are written in love. We fight a battle, not with flesh and blood, but against spiritual forces of wickedness[2] that seek to keep us from the kingdom of God.

In the last moments of time, as the final message of mercy is rejected by those who choose to worship their created objects instead of their Creator, terrible judgments are poured out on the earth.

When the literal Israelites were brought out of literal slavery, horrible plagues fell upon those who opposed the people of God. So it will be in the end of time. Spiritual Israel will be ransomed from spiritual bondage at the coming of our Lord and Savior Jesus Christ. Yet just before that time, seven plagues will fall upon those who oppose the God who created the heavens, earth, seas and fountains of waters, and those who receive the plagues will persecute the people who remain faithful to the Creator.

Please notice the sequence of the plagues, where they will be poured out, and who they will affect. These are found in the book of Revelation, the sixteenth chapter. All of the plagues come forth from heaven. The first plague will fall upon the earth, and a foul and loathsome sore comes upon the men who have

---

1 *II Corinthians 13:8, 11, 14*

2 *Ephesians 6:12*

the mark of the beast and those who worship his image.[3] The second plague is poured out on the sea, and it becomes blood as of a dead man; and every living creature in the sea died.[4] The third plague is poured out on the rivers and springs of water, and they become blood.[5]

Beloved, the first three plagues come from heaven and affect the earth, the sea, and the rivers and fountains of waters. Why? These are the elements of creation mentioned in the warning message of the first angel we looked at earlier. Also, the fourth commandment, regarding the holiness of the seventh-day Sabbath, teaches us to keep this day holy in honor of Him who made the heavens, the earth, the sea, and all that is in them.[6] The first three plagues fall on the people who reject the seventh-day Sabbath of the Creator. As foretold by the third angel's message, these are the people who have chosen to receive the mark of the beast.

O what an awful time it will be when the plagues are being poured out upon this planet! Many will be weeping and gnashing their teeth,[7] wailing because they are being justly punished for their iniquities. Yet it will be said in that time of terrible trauma, You are righteous, O Lord, the One who is and who was and who is to be, because You have judged these things. For they have shed the blood of saints and prophets, and You have given them blood to drink. For it is their just due. And I heard another from the altar saying, Even so, Lord God Almighty, true and righteous are Your judgments.[8] The hour of His judgment has come,[9] and been completed. God's verdict is true and faithful.

The next plague is poured out on the sun, and men will be scorched with fire and great heat. They will blaspheme the name of God who has power over these plagues; and they will not repent and give Him glory.[10] This fourth plague falls on the sun and scorches men with a horrible heat because men made the sun their object of worship in

3 Revelation 16:2
4 Revelation 16:3
5 Revelation 16:4
6 Exodus 20:11
7 Matthew 13:41-43
8 Revelation 16:5-7
9 Revelation 14:7
10 Revelation 16:8, 9

defiance of the commandment to worship their Creator.

The fifth plague is poured out on the throne of the beast, and his kingdom becomes full of darkness; and they gnaw their tongues because of the pain. They blaspheme the God of heaven because of their pains and their sores, and do not repent of their deeds.[11] When men choose to worship a created object - the sun - instead of their Creator, He gives them darkness instead of light. Remember, fellow believers, that the sun was not created by God until three days after the creation of light.[12] Poor, deluded souls will sit in darkness and gnaw their tongues in pain because they used them in blasphemy against the God of heaven. The glossolalia which escapes their lips is nothing more than a confused form of self-adulation, and it honors no one except the original apostate, the star of the morning, the sun god, Lucifer.[13]

The sixth plague will be poured out on the great river Euphrates, and its water will be dried up, so that the way of the kings from the east might be prepared. And three unclean spirits like frogs come out of the mouth of the dragon, out of the mouth of the beast, and out of the mouth of the false prophet. For they are spirits of demons, performing signs, which go out to the kings of the earth and of the whole world, to gather them to the battle of that great day of God Almighty.[14]

The unclean spirits like frogs that come out of the mouth of the dragon [Satan], the beast [the son of Satan], and the false prophet [the unholy spirit], are what unite these powers together. The emotional experience shared by those who have these ecstatic manifestations causes them to unite their spiritual and secular powers to promote their political agenda. They will gather together under the banner of blasphemous Babylon in preparation for their destruction.

The literal river Euphrates flowed right through the middle of the literal city of Babylon, providing the city with its

11 Revelation 16:10, 11
12 Genesis 1:14-19; 3-5
13 Isaiah 14:12

14 Revelation 16:13-14

source of life and strength. It provided the Babylonians with their water for drinking and irrigated their food supply. Without the Euphrates flowing through the city of Babylon, those whose lives depended upon her for their existence would soon be cut off.

Here is another parallel between literal Babylon and spiritual Babylon. According to Bible prophecy, water is a symbol for peoples, multitudes, nations, and tongues.[15] Spiritual Babylon, the masterpiece of deception crafted by Satan, is headed on earth by the son of perdition,[16] the Papacy, and supported by those apostate churches that reject the truth of Scripture for the lies of demons. The flood of popular support is what enables this crafty deception to survive and prosper. The people who worship under this spell of confusion are the life-giving waters that flow through the center of spiritual Babylon.

However, after the first five plagues fall upon the people who have supported this blasphemous system of

worship, they will realize that they have been duped by their leaders. They discover, too late, that the small group who cling to the commandments of God and the faith of Jesus[17] follow the way, the truth, and the life.[18] Too late the people come to understand that they were led astray by their priests, pastors, and religious gurus. No longer will they seek to persecute the people of God. Instead, they will turn against their blind guides and in a rage of fury that is exponentially compounded by the knowledge that they are eternally lost, the masses will devour the leaders of Babylon. The waters of Babylon – the people who supported this mass of confusion - will dry up to prepare the way for the coming of the Savior and His army of angels.

Then the seventh plague was poured out, and a loud voice came out of the temple of heaven, from the throne, saying, It is done!

And there were noises and thunderings and lightnings; and there was a great earthquake,

15 Revelation 17:15
16 II Thessalonians 2:3
17 Revelation 14:12
18 John 14:6

such a mighty and great earthquake as had not occurred since men were on the earth. Now the great city was divided into three parts, and the cities of the nations fell. And great Babylon was remembered before God, to give her the cup of the wine of the fierceness of His wrath. Then every island fled away, and the mountains were not found. And great hail from heaven fell upon men, each hailstone about the weight of a talent. Men blasphemed God because of the plague of the hail, since that plague was exceedingly great.[19]

He who has known the end from the beginning is waiting for the day when He can declare, It is done! Our heavenly Father longs for all of His children to be gathered into His kingdom. Yet He must wait, patiently wait, the fulfillment of His plan.

Fellow pilgrims en route to the heavenly city, the Bible declares that Babylon will fall. She is fallen; she will fall. The system of mingling truth with error begun by Lucifer in the courts of heaven will come to a final end. Babylon will be destroyed, and when she is, all of the earth will be shaken.

My brethren, the plagues are poured out upon those who reject the three angels' messages. The first angel declares that we must worship the only true God, our Creator. We should honor Him who made the heaven, the earth, the seas, and the fountains of water, and rested on His holy Sabbath. Those who do not obey the commandments of God, but instead worship a created object receive the first four plagues. The second angel proclaims that Babylon is fallen, and indeed she is spiritually fallen at this time. Lying spirits that masquerade as a gift from heaven occupy her realm. But the Word of God is clear: those who remain in this state of confusion will gnaw their tongues for pain and sit in darkness. Once this happens, those that have the mark of the beast and are suffering under the torment of the plagues will realize that they have been misled. The literal downfall of Babylon will be at the hands of those who formerly supported

---

19 *Revelation 16:17-21*

this system of deception. Those who were the pawns of this Satanic charade will ultimately be sentenced to the lake of fire. The three angels' messages are true, and those that ignore or reject them do so at the peril of their eternal life.

Truly, the times of ignorance God overlooked, but now commands all men everywhere to repent.[20] For if we sin willfully after we have received the knowledge of the truth, there no longer remains a sacrifice for sins, but a certain fearful expectation of judgment, and fiery indignation which will devour the adversaries.[21] Repent therefore and be converted, that your sins may be blotted out, so that times of refreshing may come from the presence of the Lord, and that He may send Jesus Christ.[22]

20 *Acts 17:30*
21 *Hebrews 10:26, 27*
22 *Acts 3:19, 20*

Chapter Eleven

EVEN SO, COME LORD JESUS!

Beloved, now we are children of God. Behold what manner of love the Father has bestowed on us, that we should be called children of God![1] Because we are His children, God has sent forth the Spirit of His Son into our hearts, crying out, Abba, Father![2]

No one knows the things of God except the Spirit of God. Now we have received, not the spirit of the world, but the Spirit who is from God, that we might know the things that have been freely given to us by God. These things we also speak, not in words which man's wisdom teaches but which the Holy Spirit teaches, comparing spiritual things with spiritual. But the natural man does not receive the things of the Spirit of God, for they are foolishness to him; nor can he know them, because they are spiritually

discerned. Thanks be to God that He gives us the mind of Christ.[3]

It is the Holy Spirit of God that reveals truth, and I urge you to prayerfully study everything that is written herein. As I told you before, so I tell you again: Do not despise prophecies. Do not quench the Spirit. Test all things; hold fast what is good. Pray without ceasing, in everything give thanks; for this is the will of God in Christ Jesus for you.[4]

Fellow citizens of the heavenly kingdom, our faith is greatly strengthened as we consider how God has seen the end from the beginning, He has told us about it in His Holy Word, and the end of all things is glorious. In this present world it has not yet been revealed what we shall be, but we know that when He

---

1 I John 4:1, 2
2 Galatians 4:4-6

3 I Corinthians 2:11-16
4 I Thessalonians 5:20, 19, 21, 17, 18

EVEN SO, COME LORD JESUS!

is revealed, we shall be like Him, for we shall see Him as He is.[5]

Now we know that the end of all things is at hand. Jesus warned us that as we witness the fulfillment of certain events, we should recognize that His coming is drawing near.

Jesus said: Take heed that no one deceives you. For many will come in My name, saying, 'I am the Christ,' and will deceive many. And you will hear of wars and rumors of wars. See that you are not troubled; for all these things must come to pass, but the end is not yet.[6]

Nation will rise against nation, and kingdom against kingdom. And there will be great earthquakes in various places, and famines and pestilences; and there will be fearful sights and great signs from heaven.

And there will be signs in the sun, in the moon, and in the stars; and on the earth distress of nations, with perplexity, the

sea and the waves roaring; men's hearts failing them from fear and the expectation of those things which are coming on the earth, for the powers of heaven will be shaken.[7] Truly, beloved brothers and sisters, we live in an era of fear and terror.

All these are the beginning of sorrows.[8] Now when these things begin to happen, look up and lift up your heads, because your redemption draws near.[9]

Then many false prophets will rise up and deceive many. Then if anyone says to you, 'Look, here is the Christ!' or 'There!' do not believe it. For false christs and false prophets will rise and show great signs and wonders to deceive, if possible, even the elect. See, I have told you beforehand. Therefore if they say to you, 'Look, He is in the desert!' do not go out; or 'Look, He is in the inner rooms!' do not believe it.[10]

And because lawlessness will abound, the love of many will grow cold.[11] And pray that your

---

5 I John 4:3
6 Matthew 24:4-7

7 Luke 21:10, 11, 25, 26
8 Matthew 24:8
9 Luke 21:28
10 Matthew 24:23-26
11 Matthew 24:12

flight may not be in winter or on the Sabbath.

For there will be great tribulation, such as has not been since the beginning of the world until this time, no, nor ever shall be.[12] They will lay their hands on you and persecute you, delivering you up to the synagogues and prisons. You will be brought before kings and rulers for My name's sake. But it will turn out for you as an occasion for testimony. Therefore settle it in your hearts not to meditate beforehand on what you will answer; for I will give you a mouth and wisdom which all your adversaries will not be able to contradict or resist.

You will be betrayed even by parents and brothers, relatives and friends; and they will put some of you to death. And you will be hated by all for My name's sake. But not a hair of your head shall be lost. By your patience possess your souls.[13]

And this gospel of the kingdom will be preached in all the world as a witness to all the nations, and then the end will come. He who endures to the end shall be saved.[14]

Then they will see the Son of Man coming in a cloud with power and great glory.[15] For as the lightning comes from the east and flashes to the west, so also will the coming of the Son of Man be.[16]

My fellow believers in Christ Jesus, you know not the burden I have for you. I weep that so many are indifferent to the things of God. So many do not truly love the truth, and sadly they will suffer the consequences of their own choices.[17] God declares concerning far too many of His children: My people are destroyed for lack of knowledge. Because you have rejected knowledge, I also will reject you… because you have forgotten the law of your God, I also will forget your children.[18]

---

12 *Matthew 24:20-21*
13 *Luke 21:12-19*

14 *Matthew 24:14, 13*
15 *Luke 21:27*
16 *Matthew 24:27*
17 *II Thessalonians 2:10*
18 *Hosea 4:6*

May it not be so for you, dearly beloved.

O that we may act upon a course to allow God to change our lives to be in harmony with His will. Yet so many will not heed the warning. So many will not listen to the voice of the Savior crying out: Come out of her, my people, lest you share in her sins, and lest you receive of her plagues. For her sins have reached to heaven, and God has remembered her iniquities.[19] The judgment of God is true and righteous:[20] Babylon has fallen.[21]

Our Lord and Savior Jesus Christ calls for all His children to come out of this false system of worship, to come out of darkness and into His marvelous light,[22] because the darkness is passing away, and the true light is already shining.[23] He who is the Light of the world[24] cries out now to all who have ears to hear:[25] Come out of her My people![26]

The Word of God is true. God is not a man, that He should lie, nor a son of man, that He should repent. Indeed, it is impossible for God to lie. Has He said, and will He not do? Or has He spoken, and will He not make it good?[27] All that I have shared from the Word of God is true.

O beloved believers, I have spoken openly to you, my heart is wide open.[28] Although your friends and relatives may not accept your decision, you must follow Jesus with all your heart, soul, strength, and mind.[29] Jesus has said that, He who loves father or mother more than Me is not worthy of Me. And he who loves son or daughter more than Me is not worthy of Me. And he who does not take his cross and follow after Me is not worthy of Me. He who finds his life will lose it, and he who loses his life for My sake will find it.[30] Be faithful until death, and I will give you the crown of life.[31] May you overcome by

---

19 Revelation 18:1-5
20 Revelation 19:2
21 Revelation 14:8
22 I Peter 2:9
23 I John 2:8
24 John 8:12; 9:5
25 Matthew 13:43
26 Revelation 18:4

27 Numbers 23:19; Hebrews 6:18
28 II Corinthians 6:11
29 Deuteronomy 6:5; Mark 12:30;
    Luke 10:27
30 Matthew 10:37-39
31 Revelation 2:10

the blood of the Lamb and by the word of your testimony, and may you love not your life to the death.[32]

The King of kings and Lord of lords, our Savior Jesus Christ declares:

I am the Alpha and the Omega, the Beginning and the End, the First and the Last.[33] I am God, and there is no other; I am God, and there is none like Me, declaring the end from the beginning.[34]

Behold, I am coming quickly, and My reward is with Me, to give to every one according to his work.[35]

Even so, come Lord Jesus![36]

---

32 *Revelation 12:11*
33 *Revelation 22:13*
34 *Isaiah 46:9, 10*
35 *Revelation 22:11*
36 *Revelation 22:20*